8/00

SIMPLY TUSCAN

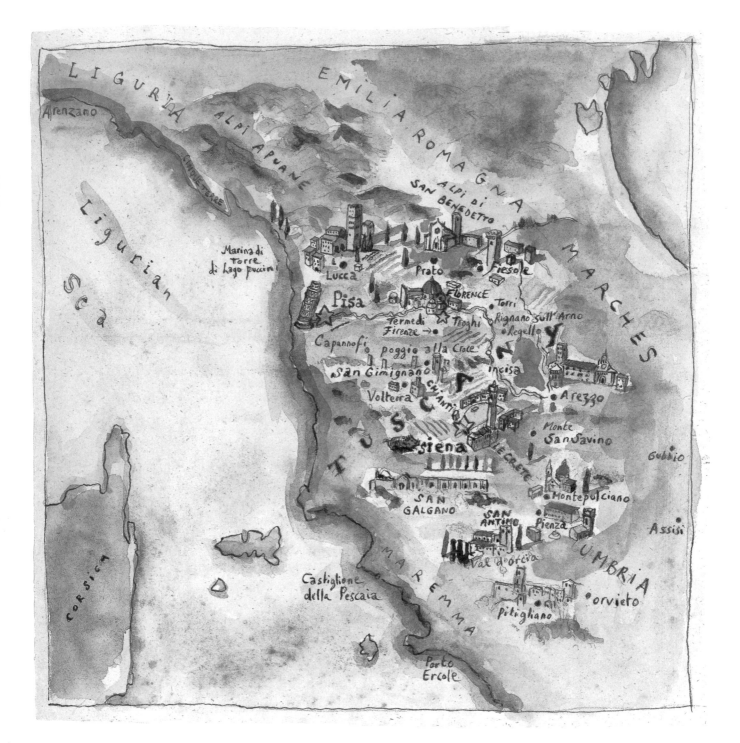

SIMPLY TUSCAN

RECIPES FOR
A WELL-LIVED LIFE

Pino Luongo

DOUBLEDAY

New York   London   Toronto   Sydney   Auckland

Recipe testing and development by Marta Pulini

Art direction by Tricia Foley

Text by Andrew Friedman

Photography by Jeff McNamara

Illustrations by Marc Lacaze

Travel provided by Alitalia Airlines

PUBLISHED BY DOUBLEDAY
a division of Random House, Inc.
1540 Broadway, New York, New York 10036

DOUBLEDAY and the portrayal of an anchor with a dolphin
are trademarks of Doubleday, a division of Random House, Inc.

Original design by S. Sandy Gim

Book design by Deborah Kerner

"To Silvia" and "Infinitive" from Grennan,
Eamon, Leopardi: Selected Poems. Copyright©
1997 by Princeton University Press.
Reprinted by permission of Princeton
University Press.

"Bagni di Lucca" from COLLECTED POEMS 1920—1954
by Eugenio Montale, translated and
edited by Jonathan Galassi.
Translation © 1998 by Jonathan Galassi. Reprinted by
permission of Farrar, Straus and Giroux, LLC.

Library of Congress Cataloging-in-Publication Data
Luongo, Pino.
    Simply Tuscan: everyday pleasures inspired
by Italy's most intriguing region / Pino
Luongo.—1st ed.
        p. cm.
    1. Cookery, Italian—Tuscan style. 1. Title.
TX723.2.T86 L86 2000
641.5945'5—dc21   99-033049
                                                  CIP

ISBN 0-385-49290-1
Copyright © 2000 by Pino Luongo
All Rights Reserved
Printed in Japan
April 2000
First Edition
1 3 5 7 9 10 8 6 4 2

To the four most important people in my life:

My wife, Jessie,

and my children,

Marco, Jacobella, and Lorenzo.

Without them,

I would be "Simply Nothing."

Acknowledgments

In the true Tuscan style, many people contributed to this book, both here and in Italy. They are:

Judy Kern, our editor at Doubleday, for her constant support and good advice;

The Antinori Family, who graciously hosted us at Castello della Sala, demonstrating a rare combination of aristocratic charm and humility;

Stefano Cinelli from Barbi, a quintessential Tuscan. His insights helped put me back in touch with the soul of the region after living elsewhere for twenty years;

Alfredo Sibaldo and his wife, Susanna Fumi, the proprietors of Osteria del Vecchio; Castello

Patrizia Anichini, who let us photograph her beautiful house in Tuscany, as well as her daughter, Anna Camilla;

Mary Foley, who allowed us to photograph her home in Connecticut, and Diane and Bob Martinson, who granted us the same favor in Bellport;

The staff of Tuscan Square, especially Lesley Whitten, Patrick Nuti, Paola Fuchs, Christina Petrelli, and Vincenzo Pezone;

Gail and Michael Racz—my closest American friends—who let us photograph their property on the North Fork of Long Island, which reminds me very much of the southern coast of Tuscany;

Everyone at Doubleday, especially Jackie Everly, John Pitts, and Michele Paolella, for their enthusiasm and marketing smarts;

My associate, Maggie Held, for her great help in keeping me organized;

My agent, David Kratz, for his belief in the project and his help getting it off the ground;

Phil Teverow, for his assistance in editing the recipes;

and the staff at all my restaurants, for their constant effort and energy.

CONTENTS

SIMPLY TUSCAN

à Saintes

Introduction

This is a book for anyone who has ever said to him- or herself, "I'm working too hard!" or "I have no life!" or "I need to stop and smell the roses." It's about how my people, the Tuscan people, enjoy themselves by maintaining an uncomplicated attitude. It's about how our deep connection to nature keeps us humble and prevents us from taking ourselves too seriously. It's also about balance—how to separate work from pleasure, and pleasure from stress. It's about looking at daily life—food, fashion, and entertaining—through the window of simplicity.

Part of the inspiration for this book was the sad fact that, for many Americans, maintaining a good quality of life has become a challenge, something they struggle to squeeze into their calendar every week. The bookstores here even have shelves full of self-help guides that tell you how to schedule such things as "quality time" for yourself and your family.

Isn't that depressing? I believe that quality of life is something you either have or you don't; it's not something you compartmentalize or confine to "Saturday from 3 to 5 P.M." And let me be clear: When I say "quality of life," I'm not talking about

exercise or counting calories or what vitamins to take. Those things you can schedule. No—I'm talking instead about such intangible pleasures as flavors, senses, emotions, and even laughs. This book will show you that these things can become as much a part of your daily life as breathing because, in my opinion, they're just as vital.

I was born in Tuscany and still consider myself a Tuscan. I eat Tuscan food most of the time, drink Tuscan wine almost every day, speak Italian to my friends, and it's Tuscan blood that courses through my veins. I have lived in the United States for twenty years, almost half my life, but I visit Tuscany every few months. Why? Because even though I adore New York, it is still somewhat foreign to me and, just as a fish left out of the water will eventually die, I need to be submerged in the elements of my homeland every once in a while or, in some way, some part of me will die as well.

But it's not just these trips that nurture me; I weave Tuscany into my everyday life right here in the United States. For example, though I'm a businessman, I never eat lunch or dinner at my desk, but always take the time to enjoy a good meal, usually with a bottle of wine, even if it's going to be a long day or a late night. When it's warm outside, I wear loafers in the Tuscan style, with no socks, even with the best suits. I don't use e-mail, especially for personal correspondence; instead, I send hand-written letters on beautiful paper that I personally select.

To put it another way, to be Tuscan is to honor all your senses. We love fragrances—colognes, scented candles, and the aroma of wine and food. Our clothing is made of lush velvet, rugged corduroy, and crisp linen. What is the sound of a Tuscan life? Opera—what else? We appreciate visual beauty in everything, from the landscapes of Le Crete Senesi, Maremma, and Garfagnana to clothing that reflects those landscapes in its earth tones, to architecture that favors flowing spaces and as much natural light and fresh air as possible, to table settings that are casual and approachable. As for taste, it's something we indulge every day by cooking and eating. I cook all the time. That's not a boast; it just happens to be something that's true of almost all Tuscans.

Is it narcissistic for me to believe that everyone could use a little bit of Tuscany in his or her life? A few years ago, I decided to find out by opening a Tuscan market of sorts in the least likely place on Earth—the heart of Rockefeller Center. If you've never been to New York, it might be hard for you to imagine what it's like in this part of the city. Philosophically, it's about as far away from Tuscany as you can get. The architec-

ture of the neighborhood is like that in most of the city—impressive but deeply impersonal and very industrial. New Yorkers in suits swarm in and out of these Towers of Indifference, running like mad dogs from appointment to appointment with pained, stressful looks on their faces.

Some day I'm going to walk around

calling out to these people: "When was the last time you took a walk in the park? Have you enjoyed a sunset lately? Have you eaten a great home-cooked meal this year?"

But, until that day comes, there is Tuscan Square.

Tuscan Square is a spectacular indoor market, unlike anything else in the United States. When you enter its doors, you don't just notice one thing, you notice everything—all at once, like the first moments of a dream. Elements of Tuscany engulf you. The room is a giant space with marble floors and a grand, spiral staircase

uniting two levels. On the landing between them is a cypress tree in a large terra cotta pot that points to the heavens. Your ears are instantly flooded with the sound of opera, which makes you feel both inspired and relaxed at the same time. Your other senses have choices: To the left, a retail space where you can breathe in the fragrances of scented candles, and purchase simple serveware and flat-ware. To the right, a restaurant, where a full menu of Tuscan special-ties awaits. And downstairs, more

casual prepared foods, as well as a bakery and an espresso bar.

The reaction of visitors to Tuscan Square—their curiosity and delight—was my other inspiration for this

book. The enthusiasm these Americans demonstrate as they discover Tuscany, artifact by artifact, reminds me of that shown by my friends after years of traveling and socializing with me: My Tuscan ways have rubbed off on them, and they have become adopted Tuscans, sharing my passion for cele-brating the simplicity of life.

I make no bones about it. I'm here to convert you to Tuscanism as well, to teach you ways of incorporating this point of view into your daily life the way my customers and friends have done. I know you can do it, because it's based on getting in touch with natural desires and pleasures.

And it's highly addictive; once you get a taste of it, there's no turning back.

How to Use This Book

Tuscan life follows nature's lead, so I've arranged this book according to the four seasons of the year. Since many of my fondest memories are of great meals, each chapter examines the foods, fashions, celebrations, and traditions of each season in the context of the occasions we associate with them. By blending recognizable American holidays and events with a Tuscan sensibility, my hope is that you will be inspired to begin "thinking Tuscan" as you plan events in your own life, from a simple family dinner to an extravagant holiday buffet.

The Menus

I've tried to blend the biggest holidays in each season with more everyday occasions. For example, the "Spring" chapter describes both lunch and dinner menus for Easter, but also includes a lunch for children and their friends, because spring is such a great time for kids. I have not provided a Fourth of July menu, but only because two quintessential Italian menus from "Summer"—a Seafood Extravaganza and a Summer Grilling and Barbecue Buffet—would both be terrific. In "Fall," there's a truffle dinner that celebrates my favorite delicacy on the planet, as well as a Tuscan Thanksgiving menu that blends Italian foods of autumn with an American holiday. "Winter" includes all the major holidays of that season: Christmas Eve, Christmas Day, New Year's Eve, New Year's Day, and Valentine's Day, with a menu for each.

All these menus are accompanied by photographs that depict an appropriate setting, so you have an opportunity to see how you might present the foods, as well as set up your home for each event.

Please believe me when I tell you that these photographs are meant only to inspire you, not to be strict marching orders. I believe that entertaining should be, above all, fun and relaxed. The last thing I want is for you to run out to the store—even my store—at the last minute to buy the exact serving platter shown in one of these pictures. You would actually be doing me a great disservice by following the book to the letter. Everything that's here is meant to be adapted freely, in the simplest way possible, by you in your home.

The Recipes

It's also important to note that these recipes are not meant to be served only on the occasions in which I have presented them. In fact, the opposite is intended. Most of the recipes are simple enough to be used everyday, and I recommend that you do just that. While you'll notice that many of the menus are intended to serve up to twenty people, most individual recipes yield four to six "normal" servings, because when you prepare a buffet for large groups of people the expectation is that each guest will sample several dishes, taking a smaller-than-usual portion of each. So, a recipe that would feed up to six people on an everyday occasion will provide enough for many more people to sample as part of a buffet.

Why do I want you to adapt my book so much? Because that, too, is the

Tuscan way. It's no accident that Italian restaurants are the most popular type of restaurant in the United States. It is because of their casual, simple approach, their (usually) low

prices and their informality. The Italian way, the Tuscan way, puts people right at ease—both the food and the setting.

The same should be true at home, for both the host and the guest. I believe that just as a good trattoria can be better than a three- or four-star restaurant, there's no need to spend a whole day in the kitchen to make a good dinner. If you read through the recipes in this book, and make some of them, you will develop the confidence to cook and improvise with little or no stress.

Improvisation was actually how many of these dishes were developed by me and my corporate chef, Marta Pulini. Many recipes in this book are not classic Tuscan, but they are Tuscan in spirit. They are simple and make use of the great foods available in the United States today. In some cases, we have changed dishes from a traditional first course to a main course, or vice versa. In others, we have replaced one vegetable with another or removed a pasta.

For example, the Ravioli filled with Pappa al Pomodoro and Black Cabbage (page 112) was inspired by the classic bread and tomato soup, which is a very thick composition made with 50 percent bread and 50 percent tomato. Here, this soup is used as the filling for a ravioli, and as a sauce with black cabbage added for extra crunch. The Seared Carpaccio with Spaghetti Squash, Asparagus, and

Pecorino (page 43) changes the classic carpaccio in two ways: First, the beef is seared to unlock its sweetness, and second, rather than arugula and Parmesan cheese, it is topped with spaghetti squash and pecorino. In the Veal Shank Salad (page 196), the leftovers of an Italian classic, braised veal shank, are shredded and served with simple accompaniments for a unique starter.

These recipes reflect my twenty years of living and cooking in the United States, the same way I hope they will inspire you to weave in your own influences as you adapt them at home.

All this talk of adaptation and spontaneity reminds me of the first restaurant I ever opened, where my goal was to challenge my diners with a simplicity they had never encountered. Since I believe that no recipe should require a full day in the kitchen, even in a restaurant, we changed 50 to 60 percent of the menu every day. We also did this for another reason—my belief that routine is the enemy of creativity. My greatest pleasure was finding some incredible food at the market and then knocking out my

customers with just one flavor. We made a lot of mistakes, certainly, but the dining experience was always memorable.

And that's what life's all about. Memorable experiences. Things don't have to be picture-perfect. But if you

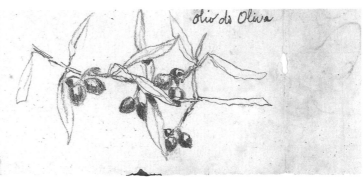

can make the experience intense, sensual, personal, and fun, you will succeed, whether preparing dinner for two or a feast for twenty.

I suggest that you explore this book as you would the towns of Tuscany—at your own pace, in whatever order you like, stopping where the spirit moves you, and leaving your troubles behind.

Simply yours,
PINO LUONGO, January 2000,
New York City, in body,
Tuscany, in spirit

ZUCCHERO

DA DELFINA

78. FIRENZE - VIA CERRETANI

CARTOLINA POSTALE ITALIANA

Fiesole - Panorama di Firenze da S. Francesco

Bacchus
Boboli

Firenze - Il Campanile di Giotto (da Via dei Pecori).

5548

Camisolles Chez Sas Souliers

‹ dai Fratelli ›

Camisolles Ch

spring

Life All Around

The smallest sprout shows there is really no death.

—WALT WHITMAN,
"Song of Myself"

I've always believed that the seasons of the year mirror the chapters in our lives. If I could choose a time for anything to begin—the opening of a restaurant, the wedding of a couple, the birth of a child—spring is the time I would select. So I begin this book in spring because it's the time of renewal and the start of life.

Spring is also a great time for you, the reader, to enter my Tuscan world by looking ahead to sunny skies and green fields, leaving the bleak gray of winter—of mundane, everyday life—in the past.

So, come on! Let's go! Imagine yourself running with me to the edge of a hill overlooking a perfectly green Tuscan landscape, a pale green field of grass through which the slightest breeze is blowing, making it look as if the field itself had a shiver running up its spine. Where are we? At my favorite place to visit in spring, Le Crete Senesi, which in the winter appears like a desert, but now seems to be painted in watercolors with big, broad brushstrokes.

I wish I could drive you here from the big city of Rome so you could see for yourself how magical it is when modern civilization falls away leaving only the vastness of Tuscany—the endless, soft hills and deep, dark woods of this region—in its place. It's very fantastic and intense, and if, as we are driving, you ask me what that perfume is that's blowing into the car, that sweet aroma that's invigorating your senses and makes you want to get out and go running through the fields as soon as possible—it's the scent of mimosa in the air.

I'm not sure what road we would take to get to Tuscany because there are two ways of entering from the south while avoiding the major interstate highway, driving instead on the old Roman roads SS1 or SS2, also known as Aurelia and Cassia.

Aurelia (SS1) would bring us in through Maremma, a route that immediately conveys an understanding of the lavish land, wild region, and beautiful coastlines that are part of the collective Tuscan consciousness. SS1 would treat you to views of unspoiled medieval towns that overlook dramatic valleys and deep chestnut forests—the most primitive surviving area of Tuscany.

As incredible as that sounds, would it surprise you to learn that if we took Cassia (SS2), you would enjoy a distinctly different but no less remarkable experience? The arrangement of trees along this route is a virtual living landscape that makes you wonder if England's legendary Capability Brown had spent some secret time here, either designing these landscapes, or perhaps borrowing inspiration for his own work in Great Britain.

I also choose to begin this book in spring because it is the time when my life began. I was born on May 31—during the Tour of Italy bicycle race, and was almost named Fausto after Fausto Coppi, the Italian bicyclist my father was cheering along the racing route while my mother was giving birth to me. Despite having only one parent in the hospital with me for my arrival, I've always been an optimist; the season, I think, got me over it.

But, whenever your birthday is, spring means that the cycle is starting all over again. At this time of year, we become like plants, nourished by the warm air and the sun, filling up with power and strength. As a child in Tuscany, I was full of so much energy, more than I knew what to do with. I wanted to explore. And to run. I would take to the countryside and run and run and run for as long as I could, until I was exhausted, which was the only way I could get myself to sit still.

So, in Tuscany, spring is a great time for children, a time of great excitement. Another reason for this is because, after the constraint of winter, it is the first opportunity to wear shorts. It's very liberating to strip off heavy clothes and have one's limbs freed up for the first time each year. When I was a kid, my friends couldn't wait to get out of their slacks and into shorts. But not me; I had a serious side and couldn't wait to grow up and begin wearing as many

clothes as possible, especially suits, which seemed very "grown up" and appealing to me.

What was my hurry? I don't know. Today, sitting in my office, I look out on the unremarkable corner of Eighteenth Street and Seventh Avenue

Simply Tuscan

12

in New York City, rather than those soft, whispering fields of Le Crete Senesi. A spring day can bring my spirits down by reminding me that I'm not as young as I used to be. The weather that used to send me running through the grass is a bitter-sweet reminder that I have to work harder at everything these days. But it's not difficult to cheer myself up; all I need to do is close my eyes and picture the vibrant landscapes of my homeland.

These things remind me that I am part of a great continuum. Even though I'm not enjoying that same energy, my children are, and their children will after them. If you can keep this kind of perspective, you can remain young forever. At least that's the Tuscan philosophy.

With the arrival of spring, we celebrate Easter, a holiday that reminds us of another rebirth. Easter is the high point of the season in Italy, where it is as much of a cultural event as Christmas. There's an air of anticipation that begins late in March and runs right through April. For my family, Easter was always the occasion for a reunion, with forty or so relatives coming from around the region to enjoy egg and bread cakes and to attend mass together.

Another great holiday in Tuscany is May Day, which takes place on May 1. This is the Italian equivalent of the American Labor Day, but with one major difference: When Italians go outside for their picnic, they take their dining rooms with them, carting tables, chairs, linens, ceramic plates, and real glass. From late morning until after sunset, the fields of Tuscany are home to the most surreal of celebrations. If you've never understood where the absurdist attitude of a writer like Pier Paolo Pasolini, or a filmmaker like Fellini came from, this will give you a bit of a clue.

These holidays sum up the blend of family, society, and environment that is the Tuscan experience. There is such openness, such tolerance, that we grow up with a confidence that is rare in the world. It's also important to note that the privileges enjoyed by Tuscans are God-given and not based on having a lot of money. From the fields of Le Crete Senesi to the picnics of May Day, the Tuscan world is open to everyone.

All of this creates a superb quality of life and a sense of belonging that goes beyond family—it makes everyone part of the Tuscan family. If you're a Tuscan, you feel at home anywhere in Tuscany. It's as simple as that.

A Quintessential Spring Menu

A Quintessential Spring Menu
(Serves 4)

Spring isn't necessarily my favorite season in which to cook and to eat—that would be fall—but there's something perfect about that first time each year when you and your friends realize that, suddenly, it's not winter anymore and say to each other, "Hey, remember that little café in the country? Let's go there and eat outside."

Eating outside . . . after months of cold . . . that's what spring is all about. It doesn't have to be more than some great vegetables, cold cuts, bread, and a good bottle of wine. The open air enhances all of it, making these ingredients seem more satisfying and complex than they would at any other time of the year. Spring eating reminds me of the Tuscan proverb, Chi vuol vivere e star bene, pigli il mondo come viene, which means, "He who wants to live and feel well must take the world as it comes." In spring, these are easy words to live by.

My earliest childhood memories are of the produce of spring. The vegetables that grow in Tuscany are simply the best. The intensity and flavor of the artichokes, asparagus, and fava beans must be experienced to be believed.

This menu pays tribute to those vegetables. The three I've just named are shown off in Fava Bean, Artichoke, and Asparagus Fricassee (page 19), while the flavor of a very different vegetable stands out in the Zucchini Blossom Risotto (page 18). Yet another vegetable dish, Artichoke, Romaine, and Pea Soup (page 17), is a study in the shades of green that flourish in the spring.

The main course here is Roasted Veal with Lemon and Sage (page 20), in which the herbs and lemon add a fragrance and acidity that soften the flavors of the dish, making it perfect for the season.

Finally, for dessert, Panna Cotta with Strawberries and Balsamic Vinegar (page 21) could not be a more fitting Tuscan ending to a spring meal. The simplicity of this custard is the perfect stage for the meeting of strawberries and balsamic vinegar, and the bursts of red will be especially refreshing after a feast that is so defined by green.

Artichoke, Romaine, and Pea Soup

¼ cup extra virgin olive oil

1 medium Spanish onion, chopped

1 clove garlic, chopped

2 tablespoons chopped fresh Italian
  parsley

1 medium Idaho potato, peeled and
  finely diced

12 baby artichokes, tops and outer
  leaves trimmed off, cut lengthwise
  into 6 wedges each, soaked in 1
  quart water with 1 tablespoon lemon
  juice

Salt and freshly ground pepper
  to taste

6 cups hot water

3 heads romaine lettuce, well rinsed
  and cut crosswise into 1-inch slices

3 cups shelled fresh or frozen peas

1 teaspoon chopped fresh mint

In a soup pot over medium heat, warm 3 tablespoons of the olive oil. Add the onion, garlic, and half the parsley. When the onion is translucent, add the potato and cook for 10 minutes, stirring occasionally with a wooden spoon.

Drain the artichokes and add them to the pot. Season with salt and cook for 5 minutes. Add the hot water, cover, and let the soup simmer for 15 minutes. Add the lettuce and the peas and cook, covered, for 15 minutes more. Remove from the heat and adjust seasoning.

Garnish each serving with mint, black pepper, and the remaining parsley and olive oil.

SERVES 4 TO 6

Zucchini Blossom Risotto

10 tablespoons extra virgin olive oil

2 shallots, minced

½ pound zucchini, washed and cut into ¼-inch dice

½ pound yellow squash, washed and cut into ¼-inch dice

Salt and freshly ground pepper

2 tablespoons chopped fresh Italian parsley

⅔ cup minced onion

1½ cups Vialone Nano or arborio rice

1 cup white wine, preferably a Sauvignon or Gewürtztraminer

5 cups vegetable broth, kept at a low simmer

24 zucchini blossoms, stemmed and blown clean, but not washed

8 tablespoons freshly grated Parmesan cheese

2 tablespoons unsalted butter

In a sauté pan over medium heat, warm 4 tablespoons of the olive oil. Add the shallots and sauté until they sweat out some of their liquid, about 5 minutes. Add the zucchini and yellow squash and season with salt and pepper. Cook for 5 minutes to soften the squash, stir in half the parsley, and set aside.

In a 4-quart casserole over medium heat, warm 4 more tablespoons of the olive oil. Add the onion and let it cook until it turns translucent, 5 to 7 minutes. Add the rice and stir to coat the grains. Add half the wine and stir until it has evaporated. Add a ladle of simmering broth to the rice and stir. When the liquid has been absorbed, add another ladle of broth. Continue in this way, letting the liquid absorb before adding another ladleful, and stirring frequently, for 10 minutes. Add the zucchini mixture and continue with the ladle-at-a-time process for another 5 minutes. Add the zucchini blossoms and the rest of the wine. The risotto should be done in another 3 minutes (a total of 18 minutes cooking time): Each grain will be soft on the outside, but with a slightly chewy center.

Remove the risotto from the heat and beat in the cheese, butter, and the remaining olive oil and parsley. If the rice seems too dry, adjust the texture with a bit more broth.

SERVES 6 AS AN APPETIZER OR 4 AS A MAIN COURSE

Fava Bean, Artichoke, and Asparagus Fricassee

¼ cup extra virgin olive oil

4 shallots, chopped fine

3 ounces prosciutto, diced

12 baby artichokes, trimmed of tops
and outer leaves, each cut into 8
pieces and soaked in 1 quart water
and 1 tablespoon lemon juice

¼ cup water

1 pound asparagus, tough stems
snapped off and bottoms peeled, cut
into ½-inch lengths

½ pound shelled fresh or frozen peas,
blanched for 30 seconds in boiling
water if fresh

2 pounds fresh in-shell fava beans,
shelled, blanched, and peeled

1 small head romaine lettuce, sliced
crosswise

6 leaves basil, torn

Salt and freshly ground pepper
to taste

1 tablespoon chopped fresh Italian
parsley

In a wide, heavy pan or casserole over medium heat, warm the olive oil. Add the shallots and sauté until golden. Add the prosciutto and cook 2 minutes more.

Drain the artichokes, add them to the pan, and cook for 3 minutes. Add the water and continue to cook for another 5 minutes. Add the asparagus, peas, fava beans, romaine, basil, and salt and pepper. Cook until the vegetables are just tender and still bright green, about 5 minutes. Stir in the parsley and serve.

SERVES 4

Roasted Veal with Lemon and Sage

5 tablespoons extra virgin olive oil

2 pounds veal shoulder (deboned and tied)

Salt and freshly ground pepper to taste

1 cup finely chopped Spanish onion

2 cups veal, chicken, or vegetable stock or broth

1 lemon, zest removed, julienned and reserved, pith removed and discarded, and pulp sliced ¼ inch thick

16 sage leaves

In a large covered casserole over medium-high heat, warm the oil. Season the veal all over with salt and pep- per, and sear the meat on all sides until golden brown, about 10 minutes, total. Add the onion and reduce the heat to low. When the onion is translucent, after 3 to 4 minutes, add the broth, sliced lemon, and half the sage. Cover tightly and simmer until the veal is cooked through, about 1½ hours. (Insert a knife into the cen- ter, and look for a light pink to white color in the center and ensure that no blood runs out.) Stir in the julienned lemon zest, and the remain- der of the sage. Cook, covered, for 10 minutes more and serve, sliced into ¼-inch thick pieces.

SERVES 4 TO 6

Panna Cotta with Strawberries and Balsamic Vinegar

3 cups heavy cream

1 cup whole milk

2 cups confectioners' sugar

1 vanilla bean, split open lengthwise

4¼ leaves of gelatin, soaked for 10
minutes and squeezed dry

1 pound strawberries, washed and
stemmed

4 tablespoons granulated sugar

4 teaspoons very good aged balsamic
vinegar (see Note)

*NOTE: Use only high-quality Aceto
Balsamico Tradizionale di Modena.*

In a heavy saucepan, mix the cream,
milk, confectioners' sugar, and
vanilla. Bring to a boil, reduce the
heat to low, and simmer for 6 minutes.
Remove the pot from the fire. Add the
gelatin, and stir until the gelatin is
dissolved. Pour the mixture into individual molds, ramekins, or small
bowls, and chill for at least 3 hours.

In a bowl, mix the strawberries, granulated sugar, and the balsamic
vinegar. Let the fruit macerate at
room temperature for at least 30 minutes or up to an hour before serving
around the panna cotta.

SERVES 4

Easter Lunch and Easter Dinner

In Tuscany, Easter is announced by bells. After days of silence symbolizing the days before the resurrection of Christ, the church bells themselves are reborn on Easter Sunday. They start up slowly, first from one church, then another, and pretty soon they are ringing all over town. It's an emotional time, because we're not used to having our bells mute, as they are in the days before this moment. Usually, they ring a few times each hour to tell us what time it is, when mass is taking place, and so on. Each one has its own rhythm and sound, and when they all go off at the same time, it's truly magnificent. In larger cities, like Rome, it's practically a concert.

Did you ever ring a church bell? It's not easy. Sometimes you have to throw your whole body into it, or maybe two people have to work in harmony just to get one "gong." I've always believed that bells are a wonderful invention made with natural materials and, even today, powered by human hands. There's something very pure about them and the way they unite entire communities. They almost make technology seem unnecessary. If we can do so much with a bell, why do we need all of the other things that clutter up our lives?

Because it's so closely associated with spring, Easter is the one and only holiday when good weather is absolutely essential. If it's raining, or even just gray, it's very disappointing and depressing, exactly the opposite of the way it should be. It simply has to be a sunny day. I think of Easter as the time of warm air and cold ground, when cherries and almond blossoms are thriving and people are eager to be out of doors in the company of friends and family.

Easter Lunch
(Serves 6 to 8)

Easter begins early in Italy. Mass takes place several times throughout the day, but the most popular time to attend is early in the morning, which leaves several hours until dinner. And those hours, like most times in Italy, are best spent eating. Many Tuscans snack on holiday foods in the late morning and don't stop until almost dinnertime—like several hours of appetizers before a big meal.

For Easter lunch, I love simple dishes that mix tradition and modernity. Not only are the following recipes wonderful together, but many of them are ideal for any time you are expecting guests over a period of several hours. This type of fare you can leave out and enjoy throughout the day.

The two most traditional recipes in this menu are the Easter Torta with Cheese (page 25), which dates back to the days when people would bring their food, including eggs and loaves of bread, to church to have it blessed, which led to them baking the eggs right into the bread. The Tagliata of Lamb with Green Mint Gelatin (page 29) honors the sacrificial animal. A leg of lamb is filled with herbs, rolled

up, and roasted. The mint gelatin is a more sophisticated version of this condiment than most people are used to; it's not sweet, but rather offers the essence of mint in a very subtle way.

Lamb is also present—sort of—in the Mâche Salad with Quail Eggs (page 30), because mache goes by the nicknames "lamb's lettuce" (it is grown in cornfields) and "lamb's tongue" (it has a tongue-like shape). This salad also reminds us of the meaning of spring because eggs are considered a symbol of life in most cultures. The quail eggs, nesting in the velvety mache and delicate watercress, make the dish look like an Easter egg hunt.

Bay Scallop and Asparagus Risotto (page 27) is the perfect thing to eat on a slightly warm, sunny afternoon. Though risotto is made with lots of olive oil and butter, this dish seems very light because the scallops disappear into their surroundings—the entire plate is a composition of white and green.

Finally, Milk Pudding with Blueberry Compote (page 31) offers a sweetness that looks ahead to summer.

Easter Torta with Cheese

For the Torta:

½ cup milk

1 ounce yeast

1 pound "00" flour or all-purpose flour
(see Note)

8 egg yolks

½ cup freshly grated parmesan cheese

½ cup freshly grated Gruyère cheese

¼ cup finely diced pecorino Romano

6 tablespoons unsalted butter, softened
to room temperature

Pinch of salt

2 pounds assorted Italian cold cuts
(¼-pound each Tuscan salami,
cacciatorino, Capocollo, and
prosciutto)

10 hard-boiled eggs

1 pound fresh pecorino cheese (aged 1
to 2 months)

1 pound aged pecorino cheese (aged 3
to 6 months)

NOTE: This high-gluten flour proofs extremely well. Purchase it in specialty stores or Italian markets.

Warm the milk in a pan or microwave until just lukewarm. Add the yeast and dissolve it in the milk. Put the flour in a large mixing bowl. Add the milk and mix until it forms a very soft, wet, and sticky dough. Add more warm milk if the dough doesn't stick to your hands. Cover the bowl with a clean towel and leave it in a warm place to rise until the dough has doubled in volume, 2 to 3 hours, depending on the temperature.

Butter a 6-inch wide, 4-inch high, round ovenproof mold and line with parchment paper.

When the dough has risen, beat the egg yolks in a large mixing bowl. Add the cheeses, the butter, and the salt and mix well, then add the dough. Knead the mixture until everything is well amalgamated, smooth, and elastic. Put the dough in the prepared mold, cover again with a towel, and let rise in a warm spot until the dough doubles in volume, probably 3 hours more.

Preheat the oven to 300°F. Put the risen dough in the oven for 45 min-

continued

Spring

25

utes, or until a toothpick poked into the center comes out clean. To serve, invert the torta onto a platter and cut it into wedges.

Surround the perimeter of the torta with some of the assorted Italian cold cuts, topping the sliced meats with hard-boiled egg sections. Serve the remaining cold cuts, eggs, and the fresh and aged Pecorino on the side.

S E R V E S   8   T O   1 0

Bay Scallop and Asparagus Risotto

1 pound asparagus

10 tablespoons extra virgin olive oil

2 shallots, chopped fine

Salt and freshly ground pepper
    to taste

6 cups vegetable broth, kept on a
    simmer

1 pound bay scallops

¾ cup white wine

½ cup finely chopped Spanish onion

2½ cups Vialone Nano or arborio rice

5 tablespoons unsalted butter

2 tablespoons grated Parmesan cheese

Grated zest of 1 lemon

2 tablespoons chopped fresh Italian
    parsley

Snap the woody bottoms from the asparagus, then wash the spears and peel the bottom parts. Blanch them in boiling water for 2 minutes, then shock them in ice water. Cut the top halves diagonally into ½-inch lengths and set them aside.

In a sauté pan over medium heat, warm 2 tablespoons of the olive oil. Add half the shallots and cook them until they are translucent. Add the asparagus bottoms and cook for 3 minutes

more. Season them with salt and pepper, and add ½ cup of the vegetable broth. Simmer for another 3 minutes, or until the asparagus stalks are tender but still firm. Process the mixture in a blender or food processor and set it aside.

In a sauté pan over medium heat, warm another 2 tablespoons of the olive oil. Add the remaining shallots and sauté until they are translucent. Add the scallops and cook for 2 minutes on each side. Season with salt and pepper, and sprinkle ¼ cup of the white wine over them. When the wine has evaporated, add the reserved asparagus tops, stir well, remove from the heat, and set aside.

In a 4-quart casserole over medium heat, warm 4 more tablespoons of the olive oil. Add the onion and let it cook until it turns gold. Add the rice and stir to coat the grains. Add the remaining wine and stir until it has evaporated. Add a ladle of simmering broth to the rice and stir. When the liquid has been absorbed, add another ladle of broth. Continue in this way, letting the liquid absorb before

continued

adding another ladleful, and stirring frequently, for 10 minutes. Add the reserved scallops and asparagus, stir well, season with salt and pepper, and continue with the ladle-at-a-time process, only using the asparagus puree instead of the broth. When the mixture gets too thick to cook without sticking, use the broth again. The risotto should be done after it cooks a total of 18 minutes: Each grain will be soft on the outside, but with a slightly chewy center. You will probably not need all the asparagus puree or all the broth.

Remove the risotto from the heat and beat in the butter, remaining olive oil, Parmesan, lemon zest, and parsley. Stir vigorously to make the risotto creamy and <u>all'onda,</u> or wavy. If it seems too dry, adjust the texture with a bit more broth.

S ERVES   6   TO   8

Tagliata of Lamb with Green Mint Gelatin

1 veal bone (the knee joint)

1 stalk celery

1 onion, halved

1 carrot

3 quarts water

1 tablespoon chopped fresh Italian parsley

2 tablespoons chopped fresh mint

1 boneless leg of lamb, tied

3 tablespoons extra virgin olive oil

Salt and freshly ground black pepper to taste

Place the veal bone, celery, onion, and carrot in a wide soup pot or casserole with the water. Bring the water to a boil, then reduce the heat to medium. Let the broth simmer, skimming the foam from time to time, until the volume has reduced by two thirds, about 20 to 30 minutes. Remove the solids with a slotted spoon and discard them. Filter the liquid through cheesecloth into a saucepan. Put the saucepan on medium heat and let the liquid reduce again to one third its volume, about 7 to 10 minutes. Remove from the heat, stir in the herbs, and let the mixture rest for 15 minutes. Filter again through cheesecloth, and chill in a baking pan until the mix-ture has jelled. Cut the gelatin into 1-inch cubes.

Preheat the oven to 300°F. Brush the leg of lamb with the olive oil and rub it liberally with salt. Place it in a roasting pan and cook it in the pre-heated oven for 30 to 45 minutes, depending on how rare you like your lamb. When the lamb is done to your taste, let it rest for 20 minutes with a 2-pound weight on top of it, then slice the lamb as thin as you can, season with black pepper, and serve it with the gelatin cubes.

SERVES 6 TO 8

Spring

29

Mâche Salad with Quail Eggs

5 ounces mâche
3 bunches watercress
24 quail eggs (or 6 regular eggs)
½ teaspoon salt
2 tablespoons white wine vinegar
4 tablespoons extra virgin olive oil
Freshly ground black pepper to taste

Clean the mâche carefully. Remove the
hard stems from the watercress and
discard them. Rinse the leaves carefully. Spin the mâche and the
watercress dry in a salad spinner.

Place the quail eggs in a large pan or
casserole and cover them with cold
water. Bring them to a boil and cook
for 6 minutes. Cool them off by
putting the pan under cold running
water. Remove the shells and cut the
eggs in half lengthwise.

In a bowl, whisk the salt with the
vinegar until the salt dissolves. Add
the olive oil, continuing to whisk
until it emulsifies. Add pepper.

On a platter or individual plates,
arrange first the mâche, then the
watercress on top. Surround the greens
with the quail eggs. Drizzle the
vinaigrette all over.

SERVES 6

Milk Pudding with Blueberry Compote

For the milk pudding:

1 cup sugar
½ cup potato starch
1 quart whole milk
One 3-inch-long cinnamon stick
1 vanilla bean, split open lengthwise
One 1-inch strip of lemon zest

For the blueberry compote:

6 cups blueberries
1 cup sugar

MAKE THE MILK PUDDING: In a large saucepan, whisk the sugar and the potato starch into the milk until it is thoroughly dissolved. Add the cinnamon and the vanilla bean, bring to a boil, then reduce the heat to low and simmer, stirring continuously until the mixture thickens to the consistency of very thick cream, 5 to 6 minutes. Pour water into and then out of a 1½-quart pudding mold, leaving the interior wet. Add the thick cream and refrigerate until it is cold and firmly set, 3 to 4 hours. (This may be frozen if a quicker result is desired.) Turn the pudding out onto a platter and rub/pinch the lemon zest over it so that the zest releases its oil over the pudding.

MAKE THE BLUEBERRIES: In a sauté pan over high heat, bring the blueberries and sugar to a boil. Reduce the heat and let the berries simmer for 15 minutes, until they are wilted and the liquid slightly reduced and thickened. Take the pan off the heat and let the temperature subside to lukewarm before serving over the milk pudding.

SERVES 8

Easter Dinner Buffet
(Serves 6 to 8)

Easter dinner calls for something special, and to me that means an incredible variety of flavors and textures that bring together the best things spring has to offer. Since this is the main meal of the season, but you still want to focus on vegetables, I suggest combining them with rich ingredients to make them more satisfying.

For example, in the Spring Vegetable Lasagne (page 35), vegetables and cheese are layered for a blend of textures and flavors that literally melt together when cooked.

A small amount of meat or pork can add a strong counterpoint to the vegetables of the season as with the prosciutto in Savory Baba with Peas and Prosciutto (page 33). Many people know a baba as a dessert pastry, but here it is presented in an entirely different way.

For a main course, lamb is a prerequisite for Tuscan Easter. Here I present it in a stew with beautiful, pale artichokes at the height of their season (page 38).

For dessert, Chocolate Sorbet with Orange Zest (page 40) uses citrus to

make even the rich flavor of chocolate more springlike. In a few weeks, it will be too hot to eat chocolate outside, but on Easter Sunday, it's a perfect ending to an open-air feast.

Savory Baba with Peas and Prosciutto

For the dough:

1 ounce dry yeast

⅓ cup warm water

6½ ounces "00" flour (see Note),
   or all-purpose flour if unavailable

Pinch of salt

3 eggs

9 tablespoons butter, at room
   temperature

For the peas:

¼ cup extra virgin olive oil

1 tablespoon unsalted butter

1 leek, white and light green parts,
   chopped

4 ounces prosciutto, cut into ¼-inch
   dice

1½ pounds shelled or frozen baby peas

1 teaspoon sugar

Salt and freshly ground pepper
   to taste

1 cup vegetable stock

NOTE: This high-gluten flour proofs extremely well. Purchase it in specialty stores or Italian markets.

MAKE THE DOUGH: Dissolve the yeast in the warm water, then combine it in a mixing bowl with one quarter of the flour. Cover with a clean towel and let it proof in a warm place for 15 minutes, or until the volume has doubled. Put the dough in the bowl of your mixer along with the rest of the flour, the salt, eggs, and butter (reserving a small piece to grease the mold), and knead with the dough hook attachment until the dough is smooth and elastic and does not stick to the sides of the bowl. Use the reserved butter to grease a 1½-quart "Turkish hat" mold. Place the dough in the mold. Cover with a clean towel and let it proof in a warm place for 90 minutes, or until the dough has risen to the top of the mold.

Preheat the oven to 300°F. Bake the baba for 30 minutes, or until a toothpick inserted into the center comes out clean.

MAKE THE PEAS: In a shallow saucepan over medium heat, warm the olive oil and butter. Add the leek and sauté until it is soft, about 5 minutes. Add the prosciutto and continue

continued

cooking until the fat is translucent, another 2 to 3 minutes. Add the peas and stir them around to coat with the leek and prosciutto. Add the sugar and season with salt and pepper. Pour in the vegetable stock, bring to a boil, then reduce to a simmer and cook, covered, until the peas are tender but still bright green, about 12 to 15 minutes for fresh peas, or 6 to 7 minutes for frozen. (If using frozen peas, use only half the stock.)

To serve, turn the baba onto a serving platter and spoon the peas onto the center and around it.

SERVES 6 TO 8

Spring Vegetable Lasagne

For the pasta dough:

2½ cups flour
5 egg yolks plus 5 large whole eggs

For the vegetables:

6 tablespoons olive oil
3 cloves garlic, chopped
6 shallots, peeled and chopped
6 baby artichokes
2 tablespoons white wine
Salt to taste
1 bunch Italian parsley, cleaned and
    chopped
1 pound asparagus, trimmed at least 1
    inch from the base, blanched
6 tablespoons butter
1½ cups water
¼ pound carrots, peeled, washed,
    diced, and blanched
¼ pound baby zucchini, washed, diced,
    and sweated in a colander with a
    pinch of salt for ½ hour
1 cup shelled fresh peas
Pinch of sugar
1 pound fresh mushrooms (morels or
    chanterelles), cleaned

For the béchamel:

¼ cup milk
5 tablespoons unsalted butter
1¾ cups unbleached flour
Salt to taste
2 teaspoons grated nutmeg
1 cup freshly grated Parmigiano-
    Reggiano

For the assembly:

2 tablespoons olive oil
1 cup freshly grated Parmigiano-
    Reggiano
2 tablespoons butter, cut up, plus
    additional for greasing pan

MAKE THE PASTA DOUGH: Put the
flour on a clean work surface and make
a well in the center. Put the egg
yolks and whole eggs in the well and
mix in a circle with your fingers or a
fork until the eggs are absorbed by
the flour. Knead the dough until it is
shiny and elastic. Put the dough
through the pasta machine as many
times as necessary to obtain a very
thin sheet (less than ⅛ inch thick).

continued

Spring

35

MAKE THE VEGETABLES: The varying cooking times of each of the vegetables require them to be cooked separately before assembling the lasagne. The easiest way to execute this recipe is to prepare all the ingredients in advance (mise en place), and then to cook each of the vegetables sequentially in the same pan, removing them to a large bowl as they are finished.

In a wide pan over medium heat, warm 2 tablespoons of the olive oil. Add 1 garlic clove, 1 shallot, and the artichokes, and cook until the shallot is translucent, about 5 minutes. Sprinkle with the white wine and salt to taste. Let the alcohol evaporate, then cover, reduce the heat to low, and cook until the artichokes are tender but still firm, about 15 minutes. Add a pinch of chopped parsley, drain, and place the artichokes in a large bowl to cool.

Cut the tips off the asparagus and set them aside for later. Cut the stalks into 1-inch lengths. In a skillet over medium heat, warm 2 tablespoons of the butter. Add 1 shallot and cook until softened, about 5 minutes. Add the asparagus stalks, 1 cup of water, and salt. Cover, and cook until the asparagus is tender, about 5 minutes. Blend the asparagus with the cooking liquid in a food processor until the puree reaches a creamy consistency. Gently stir in the asparagus tips and set the puree aside in a large bowl.

In a skillet over medium heat, warm 2 tablespoons of the butter. Add 1 shallot and the carrots and cook until the shallot is translucent, about 5 minutes. Season with salt. Set aside in a large bowl.

In a skillet over medium heat, warm 2 tablespoons of the olive oil. Add 1 shallot, 1 garlic clove, and the zucchini, and cook until the shallot is translucent, about 5 minutes. Add salt. Finish by adding a pinch of parsley, then set aside in the large bowl.

In a skillet over medium heat, warm 2 tablespoons of the butter. Add 1 shallot and the peas, and cook until the shallot is translucent, about 5 minutes. Add ¹/₂ cup of water, a pinch of sugar, and salt. Cook until the peas are soft but still bright green, about 5 to 7 minutes. Drain and set aside in the large bowl.

In a large, heavy skillet over high heat, warm 2 tablespoons of olive oil. Add 1 shallot and 1 garlic clove and sauté until the shallot turns translucent, about 5 minutes. Add the mushrooms and salt and sauté, shaking the pan occasionally, until the mushrooms are cooked but not soft, about 5 minutes. Stir in a pinch of parsley, scrape up the browned bits with a wooden spoon, and set the mushrooms aside in the large bowl.

MAKE THE BÉCHAMEL: In a saucepan, heat the milk until hot but not boiling. In a separate pan, melt the butter over low heat. When the butter has melted, add the flour, stirring constantly with a wooden spoon until it is absorbed completely into the butter, about 2 minutes. Remove the pan from the heat and add the milk very, very slowly, stirring continuously, until the mixture is homogenous, about 3 minutes. Add salt, the nutmeg, and 1 cup of the cheese. Taste and correct for salt. Set aside 1 cup of the béchamel and divide the rest into 6 equal parts. Mix a portion of the vegetables with each of the 6 portions of béchamel.

ASSEMBLE THE LASAGNE: Grease the bottom of an 11 × 10-inch lasagne pan with butter. Preheat the oven to 400°F.

Bring a large pot of salted water to a boil and add the olive oil. Cut the pasta in wide strips that will fit the pan edge to edge. Blanch the pasta strips in the boiling water. Drain each strip individually and place the strips in a bowl of ice water. Dry the strips on a kitchen towel.

Spread about 2 tablespoons of the plain béchamel over the bottom of the greased lasagne pan. Line the bottom of the pan with pasta strips. Spread one of the vegetable and béchamel mixtures over the pasta, sprinkle some of the cheese over the vegetables, and cover with another layer of pasta strips. Continue this layering process until all the vegetables have been used. Top with a layer of pasta, spread the remaining plain béchamel over the top, sprinkle with the remaining cheese, and dot the top with small bits of the butter.

Place the lasagne in the preheated oven and bake for 15 to 20 minutes, until a light golden crust forms on the top.

SERVES 6 TO 8

Lamb Stew with Artichokes

½ cup extra virgin olive oil

2 whole cloves garlic

2 sprigs fresh rosemary

2 pounds lamb stew meat (leg or
shoulder), cut into 1-inch cubes

Salt and freshly ground pepper
to taste

2 cups lamb, veal, or chicken stock,
plus 1 cup if needed (See recipe)

12 baby artichokes, tops and outer
leaves trimmed off, cut into 4 to 6
pieces each, and soaked in 2 quarts
water combined with the juice of 1
lemon

1 tablespoon fresh thyme leaves

1 bay leaf

Grated zest of 1 lemon

In a wide, lidded casserole over medium-high heat, warm the olive oil. Add the garlic and rosemary sprigs and cook until the garlic turns golden, about 3 minutes. Turn the heat up to high and add the lamb. Sear on all sides. Season with salt and pepper. Reduce the heat to low, add 2 cups of the stock, cover, and simmer for about 30 minutes, until the lamb is tender, adding a little stock if necessary to keep the lamb three quarters covered with liquid. Drain the artichokes and add them to the pot, along with the thyme and bay leaf. Cook for 10 to 15 minutes, or until the artichokes are tender. Add the lemon zest, cook for 2 minutes more, and serve.

SERVES 6 TO 8

Fresh Mixed Berries with Sabayon Brûlée

10 egg yolks

½ cup granulated sugar

½ cup moscato wine (or dry marsala or Vin Santo)

4 cups cleaned strawberries

2 cups cleaned blackberries

2 cups cleaned raspberries

3 cups cleaned blueberries

½ cup brown sugar

In the top of a double boiler, whisk the egg yolks, granulated sugar, and wine over simmering (but not boiling) water, until the mixture becomes frothy and thick, about 6 to 7 minutes.

Mix the berries together, then put them on a concave ovenproof platter or concave ovenproof plates. Pour the sabayon over the fruit, sprinkle the brown sugar on top, and put the plate(s) under the broiler just until the surface browns, about 30 seconds. (Watch carefully to avoid burning!)

SERVES 10

Spring

39

Chocolate Sorbet with Orange Zest

3½ ounces bittersweet chocolate,
   grated or in small chunks
1 cup butter, at room temperature
2 cups sugar
4 cups water
⅓ cup potato starch
2 cups unsweetened cocoa
Grated zest of 2 oranges

Place the chocolate and the butter in a bowl and set the bowl over simmering water until the chocolate melts.

In a saucepan over low heat, dissolve the sugar in 3½ cups of the water, stirring carefully with a whisk to avoid lumps. Add the remaining ½ cup of water with the potato starch to the syrup and cook on low heat until the mixture begins to thicken, about 3 minutes after it first boils. Cool the mixture to room temperature.

Put the cocoa in a bowl and slowly add the syrup, stirring constantly with a whisk to avoid lumps. Fold in the melted chocolate and the orange zest, mixing until homogenous, then process in an ice cream machine according to the manufacturer's instructions.

SERVES 10

First Dinner with the In-Laws
(Serves 6)

If there's one occasion young men in this country take too seriously, it's meeting their future in-laws. My advice to suitors who want to win over these potential skeptics is to relax and cook them a great meal—make it an opportunity to show you have taste, sophistication, and are a master of the art of conversation. If you can entertain them properly, you'll win their hearts.

While there will probably only be four of you at dinner, this menu is designed to serve six. Maybe you want to invite your own parents, so hers will understand your faults. Or maybe some friends, to show them what a nice guy you are. Or maybe you just want her mother and father to know you aren't cheap!

What are you going to talk about at this dinner? The food, that's what! For starters, there's a Seared Carpaccio with Spaghetti Squash, Asparagus, and Pecorino (page 43)—a real conversation piece because of its complexity. The sweetness of the beef and the squash contrast magnificently with the fresh, crunchy asparagus and the salty cheese. If you're particularly shy, you can make these ingredients the topping for a bruschetta by placing them on toast points, and get people talking about your food as soon as they walk in. (This change also illustrates my belief in the adaptability of these recipes, and you'll find that many of the recipes in the book can be changed to fit any occasion.)

Get everyone seated and serve them a soup, or minestra, of zucchini (page 44). Here, it's served with zucchini chips. Not only will this prove you're clever in the kitchen, but using the zucchini two ways will demonstrate that you're not wasteful, something that will be reassuring to her parents.

You also want them to know that you respect tradition, but have something of the nonconformist in you. The Ricotta Ravioli with Osso Buco Gremolata (page 46) will do just that because the lemon zest is an unconventional but striking addition that actually improves the traditional combination of rich osso buco sauce and gremolata.

For dessert, an Upside Down Warm Apple Tart (page 48). Why upside down? Because that's how their daughter makes you feel!

Even if they don't love you, they'll go home impressed with your talent and knowing that their daughter will be well fed for the rest of her life.

Seared Carpaccio with Spaghetti Squash, Asparagus, and Pecorino

½ pound beef top round or tenderloin roast, trimmed and tied

Salt and freshly ground pepper to taste

2 tablespoons chopped mixed fresh herbs, such as rosemary, thyme, and sage

6 tablespoons olive oil

1 spaghetti squash, halved lengthwise

½ pound thin asparagus, tough section on base of stalks snapped off

8 tablespoons coarsely chopped walnuts

3 ounces Pecorino Romano cheese, shaved into thin slices

continued

Season the meat by rubbing it with salt, pepper, and the chopped herbs. In a heavy skillet over high heat, warm 1 tablespoon of the olive oil. When the oil is very hot, add the meat. Sear it on all sides for just under a minute per side. Remove the meat from the pan and let it cool. Wrap it tightly in foil or plastic wrap and put it in the freezer for about an hour, or until the beef is very firm but not frozen.

In a large pot fitted with a perforated steamer, steam the squash for 25 minutes. Let it cool. When cool enough to handle, remove the inside of the squash using lengthwise movements with a fork. It will look like spaghetti.

In a pot of salted water, blanch the asparagus until just tender, about 3 minutes, then slice the stalks diagonally into ½-inch lengths. In a large bowl, mix the squash with the asparagus, the walnuts, 3 tablespoons of the olive oil, and salt and pepper.

Slice the firmed-up beef across the grain into very thin, broad sheets, using a thin-bladed slicing knife or a mandolin. Cover 6 plates with a single layer of the thin slices of beef. Drizzle each plate with a teaspoon of olive oil. Divide the salad among the plates, making a small, compact mound in the center. Top the salad mounds with the shaved Pecorino Romano cheese.

SERVES 6

Zucchini Soup with Mint

¼ cup extra virgin olive oil

2 cups finely chopped Spanish onion

1 pound Idaho potatoes, peeled and cut into ¼-inch dice

Salt to taste

3 pounds zucchini, washed, trimmed, and cut into ½-inch dice

10 fresh mint leaves

10 fresh basil leaves

Leaves from half a bunch of Italian parsley

In a soup pot over medium heat, warm half the olive oil. Add the onions and cook until they're translucent, about 5 minutes. Stir in the potatoes. After 2 minutes, season with salt and add enough water to cover the potatoes and onions. Simmer for 10 minutes, then add the zucchini. Add an additional ½ cup of water, cover, and continue simmering until the zucchini is cooked through, about 5 minutes. Remove from the heat and add the herbs. Puree in batches, or in its entirety, using a food processor or an immersion blender. Use the remaining olive oil to keep the puree from becoming too thick while blending. Serve immediately.

SERVES 6

Crispy Zucchini

The following recipe may be used to create an attractive garnish for this soup.

3 unblemished small zucchini
½ pound flour
1 quart vegetable oil, for frying
Salt to taste

Wash the zucchini well, dry them, and cut them into ⅛-inch-thick rounds. Dredge them in the flour, then shake off the excess (a strainer or colander is a good utensil to use for this purpose).

In a deep saucepan over medium-high heat, warm the oil until it reaches 375°F. A drop of water will crackle and splutter in the oil. Fry the zucchini slices in the hot oil until they are golden and crispy (fry them in small batches so you don't crowd the pan or reduce the temperature of the oil). Lift them out with a slotted spoon or a skimmer as they are done and let the excess oil drain off by placing them on paper towels. Sprinkle very lightly with salt.

Ricotta Ravioli with Osso Buco Gremolata

For the pasta dough:

2½ cups flour
4 eggs

For the filling:

1 pound ricotta cheese
8 ounces mascarpone cheese
½ cup grated Parmesan cheese
2 eggs
1 teaspoon grated lemon zest
2 pinches of grated nutmeg
Salt and white pepper to taste

For the osso buco sauce:

4 tablespoons butter
2 tablespoons olive oil
½ cup finely diced celery
½ cup finely diced carrot
½ cup finely diced onion
1 pound veal boneless shoulder,
    trimmed and diced into ¼-inch cubes
1 cup white wine
Salt and freshly ground white pepper
    to taste
1 tomato, peeled, seeded, and chopped
2 cups chicken stock, broth, or bouillon

For the gremolata:

1 sprig fresh rosemary
2 cloves garlic
Grated zest of 1 orange
Grated zest of 2 lemons

For tossing:

4 tablespoons butter
4 tablespoons freshly grated Parmesan
    cheese

MAKE THE DOUGH: On a clean, smooth surface, mound the flour and make a well in the center. Add the eggs and mix the flour into the center with a fork, a little at a time, until all the flour has been absorbed. Knead with your hands until the dough is elastic. Make a thin sheet (less than ⅛ inch) by passing the dough through the pasta machine, or using a rolling pin, as many times as necessary.

MAKE THE FILLING: Mix the ricotta and mascarpone cheeses together and add to them the Parmesan, eggs, grated lemon zest, nutmeg, salt, and pepper until the mixture is well blended.

MAKE THE RAVIOLI: Lay the pasta sheet out so that at least half of it is flat. Place a teaspoon of filling at 2-inch intervals over half of the sheet. A pastry bag is the easiest way to do this, but you can use a spoon instead. Fold the other half of the sheet over the half with the filling, and press with your fingers all over, to make sure there is no air trapped between the sheets. With a cookie cutter, cut the sheets into 2-inch rounds, with the filling centered in each round.

MAKE THE SAUCE: In a wide, heavy casserole with a snug-fitting lid, over medium-low heat, melt 3 tablespoons of the butter and 2 tablespoons of the olive oil. Add the celery, carrot, and onion, and cook until golden, about 5 minutes, stirring occasionally. Add the diced veal and cook until brown. Add the wine and salt and pepper. When the wine evaporates, add the tomato and the chicken stock and simmer, covered, for 30 minutes. (Check occasionally, adding more stock or water if the mixture begins to stick to the bottom of the pan.) The sauce should be very juicy. When ready to serve, add the gremolata (see below) and correct the seasoning with salt.

continued

MAKE THE GREMOLATA: Chop the garlic and rosemary fine with the orange
and lemon zest.

ASSEMBLE: In a pot of boiling
salted water, cook the ravioli until
they float, about 5 minutes. Remove
the ravioli with a slotted spoon to a

bowl in which you have placed the butter and Parmesan cheese. Mix gently to
melt the butter, making sure not to
break the ravioli. Arrange the buttered ravioli on warm plates. Spoon
some of the sauce over each serving.

SERVES 6 TO 8

Upside Down Warm Apple Tart

For the dough:

1 cup "00" flour (see Note), or use
    all-purpose flour as a substitute
5 tablespoons butter, at room
    temperature
Pinch of salt
2 tablespoons cold water

For the tart:

2 pounds apples (preferably renette;
    Golden Delicious can substitute)
12 tablespoons butter
½ cup sugar

To serve:

Vanilla ice cream (optional)
12 tablespoons Calvados (optional)

NOTE: This high-gluten flour proofs
extremely well. Purchase it in specialty stores or Italian markets.

Mix all the dough ingredients
together to obtain a soft dough. Do
not overwork the dough. You may mix
the dough in the food processor—just
pulse until the ingredients are mixed.
Wrap the dough in plastic and refrigerate it for 30 minutes.

Preheat the oven to 325°F. Peel and core the apples, then cut each one into 8 wedges. Using half the butter, grease the bottom of a 10-inch by 2-inch no-stick cake pan. Sprinkle 5 tablespoons of the sugar evenly over the butter. Arrange the apple wedges on the sugared butter, evenly and in one layer. Put the pan on the stove, over medium heat, and cook until the sugar caramelizes, about 15 minutes. Remove the pan from the heat, sprinkle with the remaining sugar and dot with the remaining butter. Roll out the dough to a quarter-inch-thick circle, and cover the apple mixture with it. Poke air holes in the top with a fork. Place the entire pan in the preheated oven and bake for 30 minutes, or until the crust is golden brown.

Cover the pan with a platter and flip the tart over onto it. Serve warm, and—if desired—top each serving with a scoop of vanilla ice

cream and pour 2 tablespoons of Calvados on each scoop.

S E R V E S   6

Lunch for Children and Their Friends
(Serves 6 children)

When we think about our own child-hood, we associate it with the summertime. But the friends that children actually spend most of their time with—the ones they know from school and play with on the weekends all year long—are often away for the summer. So spring is really the best time to let your kids entertain their friends.

This menu is inspired by something very simple—a desire to indulge my children as much as possible. It's not healthy, except that it's healthy to enjoy your food and not take it too seriously once in a while. This is true even for children, whom we are looking out for most of the time.

Keep in mind that most of these dishes are not seasonal, so if you're in the mood to treat your kids to something special at any time of year, they will probably love any dish on this menu by itself.

We gave this party at the home of Patrizia Anichini, in honor of her daughter, Anna Camilla, and her niece, Julia. Patrizia is a designer who lives in an old converted farmhouse nestled in the hills outside Florence. But even though we served this meal in Italy, I can't think of a child on the planet who wouldn't love it.

To begin with, there's pizza. Children in America might love pizza even more than kids in Italy. When my family goes out to dinner, we have to go to a restaurant that serves pizza, because that's all our kids eat, even at my restaurants. The Pizza Margherita (page 52) is the simplest version, but you can dress it up with your son's or daughter's favorite ingredients. At home, we let the children help make the pizza by stretching the dough and sprinkling the cheese. You should let your kids do this too, especially if they have friends coming over; they'll take an extra pride in having cooked themselves.

Mozzarella in Carrozza (page 54)

is mozzarella fried in bread crumbs, which was one of my favorite treats as a child. It's probably known to you as an adult finger food—maybe something you've had at a bar during Happy Hour. But kids love fried food and dairy products, too, and this carbohydrate-heavy treat is no exception.

The Three-Color Fusilli with Four Cheeses (page 56) sounds richer than it is. The cheeses (fontina, Parmesan, provolone, and Gruyère) are all very mellow, which makes the dish tasty without being too creamy.

And what could make a child happier than two desserts? While the Vanilla Cream Pudding with Chocolate Rice Krispies (page 59) is a rich and decadent rice pudding, the real treasure here is the Bomboloni (page 57). When I was a kid, I would help my mother cut the dough for this dessert, and then watch as she fried it up. One of my favorite smells in the world was the sweet aroma of yeast, vanilla, sugar, and dough that would fill our

home. My mother made mountains of bomboloni at a time, but would only let me eat three or four before locking them away.

How important do I consider bomboloni to Tuscan culture? When I was interviewing pastry chefs for Tuscan Square, if a candidate didn't know how to make them, the interview was over.

There's one other reason why it makes sense to serve such a rich meal to a group of children: Even the most energetic child will be wiped out by the "feast" when you're ready for the party to be over.

Pizza Margherita

For the dough:

4 cups flour ("00" if available,
   otherwise, all-purpose flour), plus
   extra for coating the work surface
1½ cups warm water (approximately
   60° F.)
¾ ounce fresh yeast
2 teaspoons salt
¼ cup extra virgin olive oil, plus ¼ cup
   to grease the pans, plus 2
   tablespoons to drizzle on top

For the topping:

2 cups tomato sauce (from canned
   tomatoes passed through a food mill)
Mozzarella cheese (2 bocconcini about
   3 ounces each), chopped into small
   cubes or shreds
6 fresh basil leaves, chopped
Salt to taste

MAKE THE PIZZA: Put the flour on a clean work surface and make a well in the center. Dissolve the yeast in a bowl with half the water. Place the salt, yeast, and ¼ cup of the olive oil in the well and, with the help of a fork, incorporate the flour into them. Add more water as needed to make a dough that is homogenous and elastic.

Put the dough in a bowl (almost double the volume of the dough) dusted with flour. Cover with plastic wrap and set it in a warm place to proof for about 2 hours. When the dough is proofed (the volume will have doubled), knead it on a flour-dusted surface until very smooth, then divide it into 2 parts and roll them, one at a time, with a rolling pin. Put them in two 12-inch pizza pans, greased with ¼ cup of olive oil, and stretch them with your hands in order to make the dough ¼ inch thick.

Preheat the oven to 500°F. Top each pizza with half the tomato sauce sprinkled with half the chopped mozzarella. Season with salt and cook in the preheated oven for 20 to 25 minutes, until golden and crusty. Serve the pizza sprinkled with the fresh basil and drizzled with the 2 tablespoons of extra virgin olive oil.

MAKES TWO 12-INCH PIZZAS

Mozzarella in <u>Carrozza</u>

One 3-ounce ball fresh mozzarella, sliced ¼ inch thick and cut into 2-inch squares

8 slices country bread, ½ inch thick, crusts removed, cut into 2-inch squares

½ cup flour

1 cup cold water

2 eggs, beaten

¼ tsp salt

Vegetable oil (enough to fill a wide pan 2 inches deep)

Sandwich the mozzarella slices between the bread slices, pressing down so that they hold together. Dip the edges of the sandwiches into the flour, then quickly into and out of the water, then arrange the sandwiches on a plate in a single layer. Pour the eggs over the sandwiches. Turn the sandwiches over until they absorb all the egg.

In a deep skillet over high heat, warm the vegetable oil until it is very hot. When it is 375°F. (a drop of water will sizzle and splatter), reduce the heat to medium and carefully put the sandwiches in. Fry them until they are golden, then drain them on paper towels before serving.

SERVES 6 CHILDREN

Three-Color Fusilli with Four Cheeses

1 pound tri-color fusilli

¾ cup diced butter, warmed to
    room temperature

½ cup very finely diced Gruyère
    cheese

½ cup very finely diced fontina
    cheese

½ cup very finely diced
    provolone cheese

¾ cup grated Parmesan cheese

Salt and freshly ground pepper
    to taste.

Preheat the oven to 300°F. In a
large pot of boiling salted
water, cook the pasta until it
is al dente. Meanwhile, put the
butter and the cheeses in a
large ovenproof casserole. When
the pasta is done, drain it and
immediately toss it with the
butter and cheeses. When everything is thoroughly mixed, bake
in the preheated oven for 5 minutes, until all the cheeses have
melted.

SERVES 6 CHILDREN

Bomboloni

1 ounce yeast

1 cup whole milk, slightly warmed

3½ cups flour

¼ cup sugar, plus more for dipping

2 eggs

1 tablespoon butter, at room
   temperature

1 teaspoon grated orange zest

1 teaspoon grated lemon zest

1 teaspoon salt

2 quarts vegetable oil, for frying

In a mixing bowl, dissolve the yeast in the milk (an electric mixer will work well for this recipe). Add the flour, ¼ cup sugar, the eggs, butter, and orange and lemon zest; mix them in thoroughly. Knead the dough until it is very smooth, then add the salt and knead for 2 or 3 minutes more. Cover with plastic wrap and let the dough proof in the refrigerator for 6 hours.

Line a sheet pan with parchment or wax paper. Remove the dough from the bowl and roll it out on a clean working surface into a sheet ¼ inch thick. Cut 3-inch circles out of the dough with a cookie cutter or glass. Place the circles, not too close to one another, on the sheet pan, and drape plastic wrap loosely over them. Let the circles proof at room temperature for 30 minutes—they will puff up and out a little.

In a deep pan over medium-high heat, warm the oil until it reaches 375°F. (a drop of water will splutter and crackle in it). Drop in the circles, a few at a time, and fry them until they're golden brown, lifting them out of the oil as they are done and draining them on paper towels. When they are cool enough to handle, dip the bomboloni in sugar and arrange them, sugared side up, on a platter.

IF YOU LIKE, FILL EACH BOM-BOLONI WITH PASTRY CREAM: Fill a pastry bag with pastry cream. Insert the medium-size tip into the center of the bottom of each bomboloni and squeeze gently to release about 1 tablespoon of cream. Carefully remove the tip from the pastry.

MAKES ABOUT 20 BOMBOLONI; IF THERE ARE ANY LEFT, SAVE THEM FOR LATER AS THEY KEEP VERY WELL.

Vanilla Cream Pudding with Chocolate Rice Krispies

5 egg yolks

1 cup sugar

2 cups heavy cream

3 egg whites

2 cups Cocoa Krispies

In a metal mixing bowl, cream the egg yolks and the sugar together with a whisk. Make a double boiler by placing the mixing bowl over a small saucepan of simmering water on low heat, and continue to whisk. After 6 to 7 minutes, when the mixture becomes fluffy and thick, and about doubles in volume, remove the bowl from the simmering water and place it in a pan or larger bowl of ice water to cool down quickly, whisking frequently.

In a bowl, whip the heavy cream until it forms stiff peaks, then in a separate bowl do the same with the egg whites. When the egg and sugar mixture is cool, fold in the whipped cream, then the egg whites, and then the Rice Krispies. Mix gently but thoroughly.

Pour water into and then out of a savarin mold, leaving the interior wet. Pour the Rice Krispies mixture into the savarin mold and chill it overnight in the refrigerator. To serve, dip the mold into hot water for a few seconds to loosen, then turn it out onto a platter.

SERVES 8 TO 10 CHILDREN.

Summer

Passionate Impulses

XIL
L'Infinito

Sempre caro mi fu quest'ermo colle,
E questa siepe, che da tanta parte
Dell'ultimo orizzonte il guardo esclude.
Ma sedendo e mirando, interminati
Spazi di là da quella, e sovrumani
Silenzi, e profondissima quiete
Io nel pensier mi fingo; ove per poco
Il cor non si spaura. E come il vento
Odo stormir tra queste piante, io quello
Infinito silenzio a questa voce
Vo comparando: e mi sovvien l'eterno,
E le morte stagioni, e la presente
E viva, e il suon di lei. Così tra questa
Immensità s'annega il pensier mio:
E il naufragar m'è dolce in questo mare.

—GIACOMO LEOPARDI

Infinitive

I've always loved this lonesome hill
And this hedge that hides
The entire horizon, almost, from sight.
But sitting here in a daydream, I picture
The boundless spaces away out there, silences
Deeper than human silence, an unfathomable hush
In which my heart is hardly a beat
From fear. And hearing the wind
Rush rustling through these bushes,
I pit its speech against infinite silence—
And a notion of eternity floats to mind,
And the dead seasons, and the season
Beating here and now, and the sound of it. So,
In this immensity my thoughts all drown;
And it's easeful to be wrecked in seas like these.

—translated by
EAMON GRENNAN

If spring corresponds to the beginning of life, then summer mirrors the teen-age years, as well as one's twenties and early thirties—when passion and impulses dictate our actions. At least that's how I think about it. Picture the summer sun and you'll understand what I mean; how can its fire not put you in mind of energy, love, and adventure? And, like any fire, it's a fleeting thing that must be savored while it's there, because it will burn out far too soon.

But when we are children, summer seems endless and vast, like our most eternal longings. For me, this is summed up by one of my favorite activities as a child—lying on my back in a field of grass in Maremma and looking up at the stars. New York is so brutally exposed to electric light that the stars are actually obstructed from view. But out in the country, where I live with my family, or on our trips to Tuscany, my daughter, Jacobella, amazes me whenever she dances off on her own and finds the perfect spot under the moon to—as she likes to say—"lie down and look up."

When I think back on my childhood summers, even the nights seem to be bright. In Tuscany, the summer fields are dotted with red poppies and white daisies so brilliant that you can actually see their colors in the moonlight. Our parents used to tell us that if you ran out into the field and lay down on top of your favorite color, it would tell you what kind of person you would turn out to be when you grew up: Red meant you would be passionate and successful; green, envious and shy; and white, virtuous and innocent. I'm not saying what color I always ended up on, but it wasn't green or white, I can tell you that!

Playing games about our future and looking up into the sky are the ultimate summer rituals, and they are definitely related. I didn't know it then, but looking into the summer sky, we are looking into the vast unknown. We are looking into our own futures.

Romantic? To be sure. And summer romance, for the most part, can be casual and spontaneous. But don't make the mistake of confusing casual with a lack of style. Many people take summer for granted, like men and women who've been together for a while and begin to become sloppy around one another. As at all times in life, it's crucial in the summer that you keep the romance alive.

This is true of all aspects of summer, meaning that it's also important to have a vision of how to entertain people in this season. And I don't mean the stereotypical vision of the patriarch hiding behind a grill. I tell you, sometimes I have only to walk in the door and see that sad spectacle to know that I'm in for a depressing experience.

Think about it! How many great nights do we have in our lives? How many beautiful, temperate, moon-drenched evenings when we actually have the time to stop and just enjoy ourselves and our friends and families? Being

presented with such a night should be like meeting a sensational person—a stunning woman or a handsome, charming man—an opportunity for a romance of sorts, between ourselves and nature.

So, when you entertain in the summer, think of it as having a date with nature. And keep in mind that nature is not shallow; she will not be impressed with fancy clothes or an expensive serving platter. You need to show this beautiful creature that you understand her. In other words, when you're entertaining in the summer, you have to learn to take it easy . . . with style.

To make this as simple as possible, try looking at summer entertaining through the lens of comfort. To me, the single most important element of hosting people during this season is to make the outdoors as comfortable as possible. When we entertain in the summer, for example, to keep everyone at ease, we forget about showing off our handmade plates and crystal glasses and just use thin plastic plates and paper napkins. We also use big plastic glasses, even for wine, so no refills are necessary. This way, when people are outside, they aren't worried about breaking anything, and they don't have to keep getting up to get more food and drink.

I think this is very important because when you're sitting in the outdoors, the generous space, the boundless environment, can lead to very meaningful interactions. This is a Tuscan dynamic, growing closer to one another as we blend into the landscape together. To me, it's a great antidote to cocktail parties and formal functions at which, I often feel, friendships just don't deepen.

For me, this kind of night outdoors is most perfect when spent with my friends Gail and Michael, who have a home on the North Fork of Long Island. There, amidst corn fields, farm land, and a convenient beach just 100 feet away, they and my wife, Jessie, and I have formed a bond that goes beyond friendship. And we've done it with the most simple ingredients—wine, food, conversation, and even silence, enjoy-ing sunsets together or stopping to marvel at a breeze as it pushes its way gently through a row of corn stalks.

I mention Gail and Michael not only because of their incredible talent for entertaining, but also because of how we met. They were customers at my first restaurant, and we managed to transcend the boundary between restau-rateur and patron, host and guest, proprietor and customer, to become friends. And it was as natural as if we had met back in school, or sponta-neously at a party. I can't think of a more powerful testament to the posi-tive forces of food and wine in my life.

Let me be clear about white wine: I don't recommend it as something to drink with a meal. Too many of these varieties have a man-made flavor. For example, most Chardonnays taste the same, oaky way, as if they would rather be red wine, but are afraid to make the transition. Sometimes I like white wine as an apéritif—its fruity, dry quality can be refreshing. And this is certainly the case in the sum-mer, when white wine is almost like an adult lemonade. White wine can even work well with fish, or in Bicicletta, an apéritif made with white wine and lemon. But in general, I like my wine the same way I like my people—bold and straightforward.

A Quintessential Summer Menu

A Quintessential Summer Menu
(Serves 4)

In some seasons, like fall and winter, the foods we eat are almost an antidote to the weather, but in the summer, the foods are a reflection of the weather; the two exist in perfect harmony. Summer is a time for eating seafood, fruits, and vegetables—sim-

ple, succulent ingredients that thrive in the heat and complement its qualities.

To begin a summer meal, you can always depend on a bruschetta. The name of this dish comes from the Roman dialect. Since Rome is just south of Tuscany, this city has had a lot of influence on the Tuscan people over the ages. Here in the United States, many people are used to being served a bruschetta of tomatoes and olive oil when they sit down for dinner at an Italian restaurant. But the national definition of <u>bruschetta</u> is simply toast topped with <u>something.</u> In Tuscany, for example, one variation on bruschetta is a <u>fettunta,</u> which literally means "oily slice," and is a disc of toasted bread topped with garlic and olive oil. Similarly, a <u>crostino</u> is topped with chicken liver. In summer, I like to make a Seafood Bruschetta (page 71) with squid, clams, shrimp, and mussels, adding some lemon zest and parsley to really bring out the flavors of those delicious creatures.

In fact, seafood is the prototypical Italian summer favorite. Many Italians spend their summers at the beach, so we associate seafood with that setting. Not only that, but on a hot summer day or night, when you're not interested in a filling, meaty meal, fish is a lighter alternative, a satisfying protein that doesn't leave you too full to enjoy the warm weather. For this reason, I've included a complete Summer Night Seafood Extravaganza Buffet in the following pages. But I've placed my favorite summer seafood dish, a Cacciucco (page 74), or Tuscan fish and shellfish stew, in this menu. It is based on a dish that fishermen would improvise, a sort of Tuscan bouillabaisse, a comparison that makes special sense because the seafood is piled atop and around a fettunta, the oily bread I mentioned above, much as the French version is built on a crouton.

Another important aspect of summer dining is herbs, whose aromatic qualities are especially appropriate during this season as they bring to mind freshly cut grass or the powerful, earthy smell of being outside. Here a Ricotta and Thyme Tortelloni with Fava Bean Sauce (page 72) brings the creamy, refreshing qualities of ricotta cheese together with the delicate flavor of fava beans. The two are combined as the filling for a small dumpling, and topped with a sauce that is redolent of thyme.

Similarly, the Aromatic Salad of Mediterranean Herbs (page 76), puts oregano, marjoram, tarragon, and parsley front and center for an intense composition of fragrances. This dish may not sound satisfying, but remember: Smell is 90 percent of taste, and if your sense of smell is satisfied, your stomach will follow.

Watermelon must be the perfect summer fruit. Its very name suggests swimming pools and liquid refreshment. Here, we've made it the foundation for a Watermelon Granita (page 86), a sweet, pink, icy confection that is as light as the summer wind coming off the ocean.

None of these dishes is selected for being the best or most complex. Rather, they are all timeless, dependable classics that lend themselves to mixing and matching as you and your guests see fit.

My favorite type of bruschetta is al pomodoro, which my mother made into an art form by slicing the bread very thick and rubbing it with fresh tomato pulp—seeds and all. Then she would drizzle olive oil and salt over the slices and refrigerate them, bringing them out when they had a nice chill on them.

Summer Herbs: Most people associate basil with the summer, but I find this to be an overrated herb. My favorites are rosemary (paired with lemon), sage, and oregano. Mix up your herbs next summer and give these others a chance.

70

Seafood Bruschetta

4 tablespoons extra virgin
   olive oil
2 cloves garlic, chopped
16 mussels, bearded and
   scrubbed
16 clams, scrubbed
½ cup white wine
Pinch of crushed hot red
   pepper
2 ounces cleaned
   calamari, cut into rings
2 ounces bay scallops
12 medium shrimp, shelled
   and deveined
2 ripe tomatoes, peeled,
   seeded, and diced
1 tablespoon chopped
   fresh Italian parsley
4 broad, thick slices of
   country bread

In a wide, shallow pan over medium heat, warm half the oil. Add half the garlic and cook until the garlic turns gold, about 3 minutes. Add the mussels and clams, cover, and cook over high heat until the shells are open, about 5 minutes. Add half the wine and cook uncovered until the alcohol has evaporated, about 2 minutes. Remove from the heat. When cool enough to handle, remove and discard the mussel and clam shells.

In a clean wide, shallow pan over medium heat, warm the remaining oil. Add the remaining garlic and the crushed red pepper, and cook for about 3 minutes, until the garlic turns gold. Add the calamari, scallops, and shrimp, and cook, stirring frequently, until they are just cooked through, 2 or 3 minutes. Add the remaining wine, and continue cooking until it evaporates, about 3 minutes. Add the tomatoes and the clam and mussel mixture, and cook for 5 minutes more. Add the parsley, stir, and remove from the heat.

Grill or toast the bread and top each slice with a portion of the seafood.

SERVES 4

Ricotta and Thyme Tortelloni with Fava Bean Sauce

2 cups flour

4 whole eggs plus 3 egg yolks

2 pounds fava beans, shelled

Salt to taste

3 tablespoons extra virgin olive oil

3½ ounces prosciutto, finely chopped

2 shallots, finely chopped

¼ cup vegetable stock

1¼ cups ricotta cheese

1¼ cups grated Parmesan cheese

Freshly ground black pepper to taste

Bread crumbs for thickening, if
    necessary

4 tablespoons unsalted butter

2 teaspoons fresh thyme leaves

To make the dough, on a clean, smooth surface mound the flour and make a well in the center. Add the 4 whole eggs and mix and knead with your hands until the eggs are absorbed and the dough is elastic. Make a thin sheet by passing the dough through the pasta machine, or using a rolling pin.

To make the filling, bring a pot of salted water to a boil. Blanch the shelled favas for 1 minute, drain, and shock in ice water. Peel the skins off the fava beans with your fingertips.

In a skillet over medium-high heat, warm the olive oil. Add the prosciutto and shallots and cook until they brown, about 5 minutes. Add three quarters of the peeled fava beans (set aside the remainder for later use in the sauce) and the vegetable stock. Bring to a boil, cook for 5 minutes, and remove from the heat to cool. When the mixture is cool enough to handle, remove the fava beans with a slotted spoon, reserving the cooking liquid. Chop the fava beans coarsely and put them in a mixing bowl with the ricotta, 1 cup of the Parmesan, 2 of the egg yolks, and salt and pepper to taste. Mix well. If the mixture is not as stiff as cold cookie dough, add some bread crumbs to thicken it.

To make the tortelloni, lay the pasta sheet out flat. Using a pastry cutter, cut it into 2¼-inch squares. Brush with egg wash (the remaining egg yolk mixed with half an egg shell of water). Place a teaspoon of filling in the middle of each square. Fold one corner of each square over to make triangles, and seal by pressing down the edges with your fingers. Fold the corners down around your finger, pressing them together so that the filled part and the wide angle corner are on one side and the two acute angled corners are pinched together on the other side.

To make the sauce, melt the butter in a saucepan. Add the reserved fava beans, the reserved cooking liquid from the fava beans, and the thyme leaves, and cook over low heat for 5 minutes.

In a pot of boiling salted water, cook the tortelloni until they float (3 or 4 minutes). Remove from the water with a slotted spoon and add them to the sauce. Simmer the tortelloni and sauce together for 2 minutes, adding some of the tortelloni cooking water if the sauce seems too dry. Serve on warm plates with the remaining Parmesan sprinkled on top.

SERVES 4

Cacciucco

Tuscan Fish and Shellfish Stew

¼ cup olive oil

1 medium red onion, finely chopped (about ⅔ cup)

4 cloves garlic, chopped

24 small clams, well scrubbed

24 mussels, bearded and scrubbed

1 cup white wine

¾ pound white-fleshed fish fillets (your choice: cod, seabass, swordfish, grouper, halibut, etc.), cut into rough chunks

8 large shrimp in their shells

Salt and freshly ground pepper to taste

1 cup canned peeled tomatoes

4 tablespoons chopped fresh Italian parsley

Fettunta (recipe follows)

In a large pot over medium heat, warm the olive oil. Add the onion and garlic and cook until they are golden, about 5 minutes. Add the clams and mussels (strong-tasting, juicy items are added before milder ingredients), and the white wine. When the wine has reduced by half, about 3 minutes, add the chunks of fish, being sure to add the larger chunks before the smaller ones, and then the shrimp. Turn the heat to high, season with salt and pepper, and add the tomatoes and 3 tablespoons of the parsley. When the whole mixture is bubbling and hot, pour cold water into the pot to cover all of the solids, thus stopping the cooking. Turn the heat to low and bring the stew slowly back up to a simmer, uncovered, until the fish is just tender. Check after 10 minutes to see if the fish is cooked. If you can penetrate it easily with a fork, it is done. Don't overcook the fish!

As soon as the cacciucco is ready, serve it in wide bowls, shells and all, over fettunta, sprinkled with the remaining parsley.

Fettunta

4 thick slices crusty Italian bread
4 cloves garlic, peeled, stem end cut
  off
1 tablespoon extra virgin olive oil
Salt to taste

Toast the bread. Scrape a garlic
clove onto one side of each slice. The
garlic will disintegrate and release
its pulp and juice into the bread.
Sprinkle each slice with olive oil and
salt.

SERVES 4

Aromatic Salad of Mediterranean Herbs

6 ounces mesclun

1 bunch of baby arugula

20 basil leaves, torn roughly by hand

40 Italian parsley leaves

16 mint leaves

2 tablespoons whole fresh tarragon
  leaves

2 tablespoons whole fresh marjoram
  leaves

2 tablespoons whole fresh oregano
  leaves

½ teaspoon salt

4 teaspoons red wine vinegar

3 tablespoons extra virgin olive oil

Rinse all the greens and herbs thoroughly, dry them carefully, and put them in a big bowl.

In the bowl of a large spoon held over the salad, stir the salt in the vinegar until the salt has dissolved. Sprinkle it over the salad and mix well. Then drizzle the oil over the salad and toss thoroughly to make sure each leaf is coated.

SERVES 4

Watermelon Granita

1 pound watermelon pulp
1 cup plus 3 tablespoons sugar
Juice of ½ lemon
Mint leaves, for garnish

In a bowl, mix the watermelon pulp with 1 cup of the sugar and let it stand for 10 minutes. Pass the mixture through a sieve or fine strainer into a metal bowl. Add the lemon juice. Put the bowl in the freezer. When the mixture begins to thicken (after about 30 minutes), whisk in 1 tablespoon of the remaining sugar and put the granita back in the freezer. Repeat the thickening and whisking in sugar steps twice more, until the mixture reaches the consistency of fine slush. Store in the freezer until serving.

Serve in cocktail glasses, garnished with the mint leaves.

SERVES 4

A Summer Grilling and Barbecue Buffet
(Serves 12)

To a man from Mars, the barbecue would probably seem like a crazy tradition. What could be more unappealing than setting a fire outside during the hottest months of the year? But those of us who know better, love the summer barbecue. We understand that it's the culinary representation of the idea: "If you can't beat them, join them." In this case, we are embracing the idea of warmth by cooking food over the most natural version of heat—a fire.

Every Friday and Saturday night in the summer, my family has an outdoor buffet. But, unlike most Americans, we never make hamburgers and hot dogs. The food we do cook, however, has something in common with those American favorites—it's almost as easy to prepare using the same basic equipment. The alchemy produced by the raw ingredients and marinades that follow will leave you amazed at the power of the grill—so much so that you may never make another hot dog!

The smoky flavor that a grill stamps on each of its subjects unites them, which allows for pairings that might not work anywhere else. The barbecue is like a rowdy party where people who normally wouldn't get along suddenly find themselves loose and easy, enjoying each other's company more than they ever thought possible.

For example, the Grilled Potato and Fennel Salad (page 81) brings together the starchy quality of the potato with the anise flavor and silky texture of fennel. But the grill moderates both these ingredients, so their qualities become comfortably intertwined.

Similarly, Grilled Scallops Wrapped in Radicchio and Pancetta (page 82) finds the bitter radicchio mellowed by the intense power of the grill, allowing it to complement both the salty pancetta and the meaty scallops equally well.

In many cases, the grill elevates classic pairings by literally fusing them together. For example, in the Grilled Figs Wrapped in Prosciutto (page 87), the figs become soft and hot, blending together with the paper-thin slices of prosciutto.

In the Rostinciana (page 83), pork ribs are almost cured with salt, which helps the fat cook out faster, then slow-roasted to yield a super-crisp finger food—a result that could only be attained on the grill. If you don't like a lot of salt, skip this one, but

if you do, get yourself a cold beer and you'll be in heaven when you eat it.

Usually, my family enjoys ice cream after a summer meal, but after a barbecue we prefer something lighter, like a soft, sensual Melon _Gelatina,_ (page 87) to clean our palates and cool us off before we go back inside.

Grilling Presentation: Grilling can leave food with a uniform, blackened look, so, when you head outdoors for a feast like this, it's the time to mix and match your most vibrant dishes and platters, replacing the colors that this cooking process removes from the food.

NOTE: There are six recipes here, not including dessert. If you make them all, even though some are designed to "serve six," you'll have enough pork ribs and monkfish to serve twelve people, as the salads do. In an everyday context, however, when serving only one or two dishes, these recipes will only serve the number of people indicated.

Grilled Potato and Fennel Salad

1 cup mayonnaise

2 tablespoons fresh lemon juice

1 clove garlic, minced

2 scallions (white parts plus half of the
green), sliced thin

Salt and freshly ground pepper
to taste

4 Idaho potatoes, peeled, sliced
¼ inch thick, and brushed with extra
virgin olive oil

2 fennel bulbs, stalks and bottom
trimmed off, rinsed, quartered, sliced
¼ inch thick, and brushed with extra
virgin olive oil

In a bowl, whisk the mayonnaise
together with the lemon juice, garlic,
scallions, and salt and pepper. If
it's thicker than heavy cream, thin it
with a little water.

Grill the potato slices on a covered
grill until they're brown and tender,
2 or 3 minutes per side. Grill the
fennel slices for 2 minutes per side,
uncovered. Arrange the potato and fennel slices in an alternating pattern
on a large platter. Drizzle the sauce
over them.

SERVES 12

Grilled Scallops Wrapped in Radicchio and Pancetta

24 large sea scallops

2 tablespoons extra virgin olive oil

Salt and freshly ground pepper
   to taste

24 whole leaves of radicchio, rinsed
   and dried

24 slices pancetta

Season the scallops with olive oil and salt and pepper. Wrap each scallop in a radicchio leaf. Fold a slice of pancetta around each packet, securing it with a toothpick or skewer that has been soaked in water to prevent burning on the grill. Grill over medium-hot coals until the pancetta is crispy, 4 to 5 minutes.

SERVES 12

Rostinciana
Grilled Pork Ribs, Florentine-Style

6 racks baby pork ribs

6 cloves garlic, stem ends removed

Sea salt and freshly ground black
  pepper to taste

6 sprigs fresh rosemary, chopped

4 teaspoons red wine vinegar

6 tablespoons extra virgin olive oil

1 medium head frisee, well rinsed
  and dried

1 cucumber, peeled and cut into
  1/8-inch-thick rounds

1 pound ripe cherry tomatoes, halved

Rub the ribs with the cut side of the garlic cloves and brush with generous amounts of salt. Sprinkle all over with the rosemary. Grill over medium-hot coals for 8 to 10 minutes per side, until fully crisp. Cut the racks into double-rib sections.

Dissolve 1/2 teaspoon of salt in the vinegar by whisking them together in a large salad bowl. Drizzle in the olive oil while whisking. Add the frisee, cucumber, and tomatoes, and toss well. Arrange the salad on a serving platter with the ribs on top.

SERVES 6

Monkfish with Caper Sauce

4 tablespoons capers in salt, rinsed
in a thin stream of running water for
an hour

6 anchovies

15 pitted green, salt-cured olives

⅓ cup red wine vinegar

1 cup extra virgin olive oil, plus extra
for brushing the fish

½ cup mayonnaise

Chopped zest of 1 lemon

6 monkfish fillets, approximately
8 ounces each

Place all the ingredients except the
mayonnaise, lemon zest, and fish in
the bowl of a food processor and pulse
until coarse, adding a few drops of
water if necessary to build up the
mass. Add the chopped ingredients to
the mayonnaise and lemon zest and mix
until smooth.

Brush the monkfish with a little olive
oil and grill over red hot coals until
it flakes with a fork, 6 to 8 minutes
per side. Serve the fish with the
sauce drizzled over it.

SERVES 6

Arugula Salad with Speck and Walnuts

½ teaspoon salt

2 tablespoons red wine vinegar

4 tablespoons extra virgin olive oil

3 bunches of arugula, cleaned
and dried

1 cup walnut halves

4 ounces smoked prosciutto (speck),
diced

2 Yukon Gold potatoes, cut into ½-inch
dice and boiled until cooked through
but still firm

Freshly ground pepper to taste

In a small bowl, dissolve the salt
with the vinegar, whisking them
together. Add the extra virgin olive
oil. Place the remaining ingredients
in a bowl and pour the vinaigrette
over them. Toss thoroughly.

SERVES 6

Grilled Figs Wrapped in Prosciutto

18 fresh mission figs
5 ounces thinly sliced prosciutto

Wrap each fig in a slice of prosciutto, securing it with a toothpick
that has been soaked in water. Grill
these "skewers" over medium-hot coals
until the prosciutto becomes crispy,
about 2 to 3 minutes.

SERVES 6

Melon Gelatina

4 pounds cantaloupe melon pulp, from
   approximately 8 pounds of melon
1 cup sugar
2 whole vanilla beans
1 cup cornstarch
½ cup coarsely chopped pistachios

Pass the cantaloupe pulp through a
sieve into a large saucepan. Add the
sugar. Cut the vanilla beans open
lengthwise, scrape the tiny black
seeds out, and add the seeds to the
cantaloupe pulp. Mix the cornstarch
with a spoonful or two of the pulp
until well blended, then add the mixture to the pan and mix well. Put the
saucepan on high heat, bring the mixture to a boil, reduce the heat to
low, and cook for 5 minutes, until the
mixture becomes as thick as soft
mashed potatoes. Remove the pan from
the heat, and stir in two thirds of
the pistachios. When the mixture
reaches room temperature, pour it into
a Jell-O mold, cover with plastic
wrap, and refrigerate overnight.

To serve, set the mold in hot water
for 30 seconds to loosen the Jell-O,
then turn it over onto a plate and
give it a jerk to release the contents. Sprinkle the remaining
pistachios over the top.

SERVES 12

Dinner for Children and Their Friends
(Serves 6 children)

In the "Spring" chapter, I wrote of how to entertain children and their friends in that season, because the summer often finds children surprisingly alone, as their friends are off at camp or traveling with their families. But for those special summer times when your children do have friends around, perhaps as house guests, this is a great meal to prepare for them.

Like the Lunch for Children and Their Friends, this is a rich, carbohydrate-heavy feast that will please the kids much more than it will the parents. But I don't find this meal any more or less unhealthy than the burgers and pizzas many children eat these days, and it's far more civilized and sophisticated.

When my kids have friends over for dinner, I use it as an opportunity to teach them about hospitality. My wife and I turn over control of the house to whatever child is entertaining, and we make ourselves their staff, acting as cooks, waiter, and waitress, serving their friends according to their instructions. Providing, that is, that they treat us and their guests with respect.

This is a very serious matter to me. Instructing my children about how to be a proper host is as important as teaching them about right and wrong or the birds and the bees. "Listen," I tell them when they reach the right age, "tonight you have invited people to spend time with you. Of all the things in the world they could be doing, they have decided to put themselves in your hands. This is a big responsibility. Are you ready to give them your full attention? Are you ready to make them comfortable? Are you ready to cook them something special? Okay, then, let's go."

Several of the dishes, or combinations, in this menu will be familiar to Americans, though in slightly different form. For example, the Chicken and Ricotta Polpettine with Pink Tomato Sauce (page 92) are the most delicate meatballs you'll ever pop in your mouth, made light as a feather with chicken and ricotta, and topped with a pale, salmon-colored sauce.

The Pastina with Milk and Eggs (page 91), is a wonderful childhood favorite in Tuscany. Pastina are tiny pasta that come in a variety of shapes, like the noodles you sometimes see in store-bought children's soups here. My daughter loves the star-shaped version because they remind her of the summer sky. I do, too.

As with our spring lunch for children, this one features two desserts. The first, Tuscan Cream Puffs (page 95) is rich and sticky, topped with powdered sugar. The second is a more sedate rice pudding, or <u>Riso al Latte</u> (page 96), which I recommend serving with fresh strawberries to keep your children in touch with the fact that, hopefully, they'll soon be returning to more healthy foods.

Pastina with Milk and Eggs

6 cups milk

10 ounces pastina (4 fistfulls) (tiny pasta, sometimes in the shape of stars or seeds)

3 eggs, beaten

3 oz grated parmigiano cheese

Salt and freshly ground pepper

Bring the milk to a boil in a large, heavy saucepan over high heat. Add the pastina and cook until it is slightly softer than al dente, and the milk is as thick as cream. Remove the pan from the heat and stir in the eggs, cheese, and salt and pepper to taste.

SERVES 4 TO 6 CHILDREN

Chicken and Ricotta

Polpettine

with Pink Tomato Sauce

For the meatballs:

½ pound ground chicken

½ pound ricotta cheese

1 cup freshly grated Parmesan cheese

1 tablespoon chopped fresh rosemary

1 tablespoon chopped fresh thyme

1 tablespoon chopped fresh sage

2 tablespoons chopped fresh Italian
    parsley

Salt and freshly ground pepper
    to taste

Flour, for dusting

Vegetable oil, for frying

For the sauce:

6 cups Basic Tomato Sauce (recipe
    follows)

4 tablespoons unsalted butter

1 cup freshly grated Parmesan cheese

6 leaves fresh basil

1 tablespoon chopped fresh Italian
    parsley

Make the meatballs, in a bowl, mix together all the ingredients except the flour and oil. Use your hands, and make sure that all the ingredients are evenly distributed throughout the mixture. Put a heap of flour in a large bowl or plate. Keeping your hands well dusted, form the mixture into 2-inch balls, rolling each one in flour before lining them up in a single layer on a floured tray. Chill the tray of meatballs in the refrigerator for 30 minutes to firm them up.

In a deep pan set over medium-high heat fry the meatballs in 5 inches of very hot oil (375°F.—a drop of water will sizzle and splatter) until they turn golden, about 5 minutes. Fry the meatballs in batches so as not to crowd the pan. As they are done, transfer them to drain on paper towels.

Bring the tomato sauce to a simmer in a saucepan, then add the butter, Parmesan, and basil. Process for a minute in a food processor (or use a hand-held immersion blender), just until homogenous. Pour the sauce into a large, heavy casserole, bring it to a boil, reduce the heat to low, and carefully drop in the meatballs. Simmer for 10 to 15 minutes to make sure the meatballs are warmed through by

the sauce, stirring frequently but gently to prevent them from sticking to the bottom. Arrange the meatballs and sauce on a serving platter and sprinkle with the parsley.

SERVES 6 CHILDREN,
2 TO 3 MEATBALLS PER CHILD

Basic Tomato Sauce

2¼ pounds ripe tomatoes
½ cup extra virgin olive oil
1 onion, chopped into ¼-inch dice
½ carrot, chopped into ¼-inch dice
½ stalk celery, chopped into ¼-inch
　dice
1 clove garlic
6 basil leaves

Wash the tomatoes and chop them coarsely. In a skillet, warm the olive oil over medium heat, and brown the

vegetables and the garlic clove until the onion is translucent, 3 to 4 minutes. Add the tomatoes and half the basil leaves, and cook for about 30 minutes. Remove from the heat and add the remaining basil. Pass through a food mill.

MAKES 3 TO 4 CUPS

Tuscan Cream Puffs

3 whole eggs plus 6 egg yolks

¾ cups granulated sugar

1½ cups flour

3½ cups milk

6 tablespoons butter, softened, plus
   more for greasing pan

Grated zest of 1 lemon

1 cup bread crumbs

Vegetable oil, for frying

2 tablespoons confectioners' sugar

In a large mixing bowl, beat the egg yolks with the granulated sugar until smooth using an eggbeater or an electric mixer. Add 1 cup of the flour and the milk, butter, and lemon zest and mix well. Put the mixture in a saucepan and warm it over low heat until it becomes as thick as mashed potatoes. Spread the mixture out onto a buttered cookie sheet with a spatula and let it cool for at least 30 minutes. When it has set, cut the sheet into 1½ by 2-inch diamond shapes with a sharp knife greased with vegetable oil.

In a mixing bowl, beat the whole eggs. Dip the diamond shapes first in the remaining flour, then in the eggs, then into the bread crumbs. Fill a pan 3 inches deep with vegetable oil. Heat the oil over medium-high heat. When it is 375°F. (a drop of water will sizzle and splatter), slide the diamonds in and fry them until they are golden, 3 to 4 minutes. Remove from the oil with a slotted spoon and let them drain on paper towels. Sprinkle lightly with confectioners' sugar and serve.

SERVES 6 CHILDREN, APPROXIMATELY 3 CREAM PUFFS PER CHILD

Riso al Latte
with Fresh Strawberries

2 quarts whole milk

2 cups short-grain rice (arborio,
   Carnaroli, or Vialone Nano)

½ cup raisins

4 tablespoons unsalted butter

½ cup sugar

1 pint fresh strawberries, washed,
   stems removed, cut into quarters

In a large saucepan, bring the milk
to a boil. Add the rice, stir well,
and cook at a slow simmer stirring
frequently, until the milk has been
absorbed, about 30 minutes.

While the rice is cooking, plump the
raisins by soaking them in hot water
for 30 minutes, then drain them. When
the rice is done, add the raisins,
butter, and sugar. Stir vigorously to
blend everything together and to break
up the rice into a puddinglike consistency. Serve warm, topped with the
strawberries.

SERVES 6 CHILDREN

Late Summer Buffet

(Serves 24)

I've never in my life considered the path of the vegetarian even for a moment. While I can understand what draws people to this disciplined way of eating and living, I simply love a lamb shank, or a roasted chicken, or a great piece of fish, too much to give them up. Not only that, but I also need the variety that the full range of food possibilities provides—to go from a salad to a pasta to a piece of chicken or meat. Whatever the effect on my waistline, I'm a carnivore as surely as I'm a Tuscan.

But, having said this, I do think people are too hard on vegetarians. They have an extreme reputation, for being either too boring or too militant. And I think this is because people who are not vegetarians find those who are a bit intimidating in some way, as anything foreign can be. And, nobody who isn't a vegetarian can believe that those who are lead satisfying culinary lives.

Well, to me, summer is the time to experiment and step into the shoes of a vegetarian, if only for one night. And what night would that be? On that one evening every September, when you think summer is over, but it comes back to surprise you, just as hot as it was back in August. On nights like this, I fight back with a light vegetarian meal that isn't too filling and leaves me with enough energy to take the heat.

As you will see from the recipes that follow, unique combinations can add complexity even to meatless meals.

Consider, for example, the layers of flavor and texture in the Black Olive and Zucchini Tart (page 105) or the Five Bean Salad with Scallions and Horseradish Vinaigrette (page 108), which conjures up a symphony of flavors.

You can also do wonders with pastas, breads, and grains, adding weight to a vegetarian dish without using meat, fish or fowl. This is certainly the case with the Polenta with Wild Mushrooms and Spinach (page 101), the Farrotto with Morel Mushrooms (page 110), and the Ravioli Filled with Pappa al Pomodoro and Black Cabbage (page 112).

After enjoying a vegetarian feast like this one, you'll have a new appreciation for the potential of a meatless meal, and may even find it easier to understand the vegetarians in your life.

NOTE: There are eight recipes here, not including dessert. If you make them all, even though some are designed to "serve six," you'll have plenty for twenty-four people. In an everyday context, however, when serving just one or two dishes, these recipes will only serve the number of people indicated. Also, if you don't have enough time to make all of these dishes, you may delete one or two and still have enough for twenty-four.

Fried Zucchini and Zucchini Blossoms

3 eggs, separated
1½ cups flour
½ cup milk
Salt to taste
2 cups corn oil
6 large zucchini, cut into small fingers
6 zucchini blossoms, if available

In a bowl, combine the egg yolks with the flour and mix well. Add the milk and salt and mix well. In a separate bowl, beat the egg whites with a whisk until they're stiff, then incorporate them into the batter.

In a wide pan over medium-high heat, warm the oil. When it is very hot (375°F.—a drop of water will sizzle and splatter), dip the vegetables in the batter and add them to the pan, being sure to handle the blossoms delicately. When dipping the blossoms, hold them by the stem and dip them into the batter at an angle—you don't want too much batter inside the blossoms. Fry them in small batches to avoid crowding, until golden brown and crisp, about 20 to 25 seconds per side, then drain on paper towels and salt sparingly. Serve hot on plates lined with small paper napkins.

SERVES 6

Polenta with Wild Mushrooms and Spinach

For the polenta:

5 cups water
Salt to taste
1 cup polenta (see Note)
2 tablespoons extra virgin olive oil

For the mushrooms:

¼ cup extra virgin olive oil
3 shallots, chopped
1 pound mixed mushrooms, such as
   chanterelles, porcini, hen of the
   wood, and shiitake wiped with a
   damp cloth and roughly chopped
1 tablespoon chopped fresh rosemary
1 teaspoon chopped fresh thyme
Salt and freshly ground pepper
   to taste
½ cup vegetable broth

For the spinach:

2 tablespoons butter
1½ pounds fresh spinach, trimmed of
   stems and well washed
¼ cup milk
10 tablespoons freshly grated
   Parmesan cheese

NOTE: Polenta is a sort of cornmeal pudding, or porridge, that is served warm or cooled and sliced, fried, baked or otherwise. Italian-made brands are sold as "polenta," American brands as "cornmeal" or "cornmeal polenta."

MAKE THE POLENTA: (Note: It is very difficult to indicate with precision the desired ratio of water to polenta. Variables such as the shape of your pot, the heat of your stove, and the variety of cornmeal you use, all have an effect upon the outcome. More water may be necessary if a softer polenta is desired. Keep a small pot of boiling water on your stove to add to the polenta if it becomes too thick too soon.) In a deep pan, bring the salted water to a boil. Reduce the heat to medium and add the polenta little by little, beating constantly with a whisk to prevent lumps. Cook the polenta, stirring constantly with the whisk, until it reaches a creamy consistency. Remove from the heat. Add the olive oil and salt. Stir well, cover, and set aside in a warm place until ready to serve.

MAKE THE MUSHROOMS: In a large, wide skillet over high heat, warm the olive oil. Add the shallots and sauté until they become translucent, about 5 minutes. Add the mushrooms and the herbs, season well with salt and pepper, and cook, shaking and stirring frequently, until the mushrooms are glistening and wilted, about 5 minutes. Add the vegetable broth, stir up the browned bits on the bottom of the pan, and cook for 5 minutes more. Turn off the heat, but leave the pan on the stove until you're ready to serve.

MAKE THE SPINACH: In a sauté pan over medium heat, melt the butter. Add the spinach and sauté it for a couple of minutes to wilt it. Add the milk and simmer until it has been absorbed, about 2 to 3 minutes, then stir in 6 tablespoons of the Parmesan.

Serve the polenta in a bowl, crowned by the spinach, with the mushrooms in the center. Sprinkle the remaining cheese on top.

SERVES 6

Garden Vegetable Panzanella*

6 slices stale Tuscan-style bread,
   crusts removed, cut into ½-inch
   cubes
6 ripe tomatoes, cut into small wedges
½ red bell pepper, cut lengthwise into
   ½-inch strips
½ yellow bell pepper, cut lengthwise
   into ½-inch strips
8 ounces mushrooms (choose your
   favorite; anything from button
   mushrooms to shiitake) cut into
   ¼-inch slices
2 stalks celery, cut into ¼-inch slices
6 scallions, white and green parts, cut
   diagonally into ½-inch lengths
6 baby carrots, peeled and left whole,
   with an inch of green stem still
   attached
Salt and freshly ground pepper
   to taste
¼ cup red wine vinegar
½ cup extra virgin olive oil
12 leaves fresh basil, torn roughly by
   hand

If the bread is not completely stale,
dry the cubes by putting them in a
300°F. oven for a few minutes, but
don't let them brown.   *continued*

Put all of the vegetables into a large salad bowl. Make a vinaigrette in a small bowl by dissolving a teaspoon of salt in the vinegar, then adding the olive oil slowly, whisking continually to emulsify. Pour the vinaigrette onto the vegetables and toss well to coat everything evenly. Sprinkle the dry bread cubes lightly with water by dipping and flicking your fingers over them once or twice, and add them to the salad bowl along with the basil. Toss again. Season with salt and pepper. Taste it—if you think it needs something, make some more vinaigrette.

SERVES 12

*This Tuscan word indicates a salad that requires the use of bread cubes and vegetables.

Black Olive and Zucchini Tart

For the dough:

4 cups "00" flour (see Note) or use
   all-purpose flour as a substitute
14 tablespoons unsalted butter, diced,
   at room temperature
1 egg
Pinch of salt
½ teaspoon baking powder
¼ cup warm water

For the filling:

¼ cup extra virgin olive oil
1 leek, white and light green parts
   only, carefully washed and
   sliced thin
¾ pound zucchini, rinsed and cut into
   ¼-inch-thick rounds (if the zucchini is
   very large, cut it in half lengthwise
   before slicing)
Salt and freshly ground pepper
   to taste
6 leaves fresh basil, torn roughly
   by hand
½ pound ricotta cheese
1 whole egg, plus 1 egg yolk
½ cup freshly grated Parmesan cheese
½ cup pitted black oil-cured olives

1 tablespoon chopped Italian parsley
   leaves
Butter, for greasing the pan

NOTE: This high-gluten flour proofs extremely well. Purchase it in specialty stores or Italian markets.

MAKE THE DOUGH: On a clean work surface, mound the flour and make a well in the center. Place the remaining dough ingredients in the well and mix everything together with your fingers just until a dough forms. Wrap it in plastic and refrigerate for 30 minutes.

MAKE THE FILLING: In a sauté pan over medium heat, warm the olive oil. Add the leek and cook until soft, about 4 minutes. Add the zucchini and sauté until it's just cooked through, about 5 minutes. Season with salt and pepper, then add the basil.

Place the ricotta in a mixing bowl and stir in the zucchini mixture, the whole egg, the Parmesan, olives, and parsley. Mix thoroughly. Season with salt and pepper.

continued

Summer

Preheat the oven to 350°F. Divide the dough into 2 pieces, one a little bigger than the other. Roll both pieces into circles with a thickness of $^3/_{16}$ of an inch. Grease a 12-inch tart pan (it's best to use a 2-piece tart pan, with a removable bottom) with butter and line the bottom and sides with the larger circle of dough. Spread the filling evenly inside, then cover it with the smaller circle of dough. Seal the bottom and top crusts together with your fingers and mark the edge with the tines of a fork. Make an egg wash, using the yolk and half an eggshell of water, and brush the crust with it. Poke steam holes in the crust with a fork. Bake for 40 minutes, or until the crust is golden brown.

Let the tart rest until it is just warm so that it sets firmly enough to slice. If you are not using a 2-piece tart pan, you'll need to turn the tart over onto a plate, and then turn it back right side up onto a serving plate.

MAKES ONE 12-INCH TART

Roasted Root Vegetables

1 carrot

1 butternut squash, peeled, seeded, and cut into 1-inch dice

1 celery root, peeled and cut into 1-inch pieces

4 small, or 2 large, turnips, peeled and cut into 1-inch pieces

4 small, or 2 large, red onions, peeled and quartered, root end intact

Extra virgin olive oil to coat the above

Salt and freshly ground pepper to taste

Mixed herbs of your choice (such as thyme, rosemary, savory, Italian parsley)

Preheat the oven to 375°F. In a bowl, toss the vegetables with the olive oil, salt, pepper, and herbs. Place in a roasting pan and roast for 30 minutes, or until brown and tender. Serve warm.

SERVES 6

Five Bean Salad with Scallions and Horseradish Vinaigrette

1 cup dry chick-peas

1 cup dry cannellini (white kidney beans)

1 cup dry borlotti (cranberry or Roman beans)

1 cup dry black-eyed peas

1 cup dry green lentils

1 cup dry barley

1 carrot, peeled

1 stalk celery, rinsed

1 whole onion, peeled

1 bouquet garni (1 sprig rosemary, 2 whole peeled cloves garlic, 2 sprigs thyme, all wrapped and tied in cheesecloth)

2½ teaspoons salt

2 tablespoons extra virgin olive oil, plus ⅓ cup for the dressing

3 tablespoons red wine vinegar

1 teaspoon freshly grated horseradish

2 bunches of fresh scallions, rinsed and cut into ½-inch slices (white and light green parts only)

Freshly ground black pepper to taste

Soak the chick-peas, cannellini, borlotti, and black-eyed peas separately in plenty of water overnight. Soak the lentils and barley separately for 2 hours.

Fill a big pot two thirds full with water. Add the carrot, celery, onion, and the bouquet garni, and put on high heat. When the water comes to a boil, reduce the heat and simmer for 20 minutes. Stir in the borlotti. After 10 minutes, stir in the cannellini; after 10 minutes more, stir in the black-eyed peas. After another 10 minutes, stir in the barley, and after 10 more minutes, stir in the lentils. Add 2 teaspoons of the salt. Simmer until the beans are cooked but not mushy, about 20 minutes. Strain the beans through a colander, pick out and discard the vegetables and the bouquet garni, and spread the beans out to cool on a sheet pan, drizzling 2 tablespoons of olive oil over them and stirring them around to coat with the olive oil.

In a bowl, dissolve the remaining salt in the red wine vinegar with a whisk. Add the grated horseradish and the 1/3 cup of olive oil and beat with the whisk until the dressing is emulsified.

In a large bowl, mix the beans with the vinaigrette and the scallions. Finish the salad by grinding plenty of black pepper over it.

S ERVES   6

Farrotto with Morel Mushrooms

For the mushrooms:

½ ounce dry porcini mushrooms

2 cups warm water

⅓ cup extra virgin olive oil

1 pound fresh wild mushrooms (pick
  what looks best at the market), stems
  discarded, caps sliced

½ teaspoon chopped fresh rosemary

½ teaspoon fresh thyme leaves

Salt and freshly ground pepper
  to taste

For the rice:

¾ cup extra virgin olive oil

⅔ cup chopped onion

2½ cups farro (see page 111), soaked
  2 hours, then strained and patted
  dry

¾ cup white wine

6 cups vegetable broth, kept at a
  simmer

2 cloves garlic, minced

¾ cup freshly grated Parmigiano-
  Reggiano cheese

3 tablespoons chopped Italian parsley

2 tablespoons unsalted butter

PREPARE THE MUSHROOMS: In a bowl, soak the porcini in the warm water for 30 minutes, then squeeze them dry and chop them coarsely. Strain the soaking liquid through a cheesecloth and add 2 cups of it to the vegetable broth for the rice. Discard the rest or reserve it for another use.

In a wide skillet over high heat, warm the olive oil. Add the fresh mushrooms, rosemary, and thyme and cook, shaking frequently, for 3 minutes. Add the porcini and cook for 3 minutes more. Season with salt and pepper and remove the pan from the heat.

PREPARE THE <u>FAROTTO</u>: In a 5-quart casserole over medium heat, warm ½ cup of the olive oil. Add the onion and sauté until it's translucent, about 5 minutes. Add the farro and stir to coat the grains. Add the wine and stir until it has evaporated, about 3 minutes. Add a ladle of simmering broth to the rice and stir. When the liquid has been absorbed, add another ladle of simmering broth. Continue in this way, letting the liquid be absorbed before adding another ladleful and stirring frequently, for 12 minutes. Add the mushrooms and con-

tinue with the ladle-at-
a-time process. The
<u>farotto</u> should be ready
in another 10 minutes.
Each grain will be soft
on the outside, but with
a slightly chewy center.
Remove the <u>farrotto</u> from
the heat and beat in the
garlic, cheese, parsley,
butter, and the rest of
the olive oil. If it
seems too dry, adjust the
texture with a bit more
broth.

S E R V E S   6

Farro: This ancient, mul-
tipurpose grain is common
to Mediterranean gastron-
omy—I'd call it the
Tuscan couscous. It's a
wonderful alternative to
bread in summer salads
and soups. Farro may be
purchased, usually in
one-pound bags in spe-
cialty stores and Italian
markets. Although, like
any grain, it has many
uses, I usually use it
in <u>Farrotto,</u> a risotto-
like dish comprising
farro and a lot of
stock, which is absorbed
into the grain.

Ravioli filled with
Pappa al Pomodoro
and Black Cabbage

For the pasta:

1 pound "00" flour (see Note), or use
   all-purpose flour as a substitute
5 whole eggs, plus 1 egg yolk

For the filling:

1 pound ricotta cheese
1 egg
3/4 cup freshly grated Parmesan cheese
6 black cabbage leaves (or substitute
   kale), steamed until tender (about 10
   minutes) and chopped fine
Salt and freshly ground pepper
   to taste

For the sauce:

1 pound stale bread
1 1/2 quarts vegetable stock
3 cups Basic Tomato Sauce
   (page 93)
12 leaves fresh basil, torn roughly by
   hand

1/2 cup extra virgin olive oil, plus 3
   tablespoons for drizzling on the
   ravioli
Salt and freshly ground pepper
   to taste
6 leaves black cabbage, steamed until
   tender (about 10 minutes) and cut
   into 1/2-inch strips
3 cloves garlic, chopped

NOTE: This high-gluten flour proofs
extremely well. Purchase it in specialty stores or Italian markets.

MAKE THE PASTA: On a clean, smooth
surface, mound the flour and make a
well in the center. Add the whole eggs
and mix the flour into the center with
a fork, a little at a time, until all
has been absorbed. Knead with your
hands until the dough has a smooth and
even consistency. Make a thin sheet by
passing the dough through a pasta
machine as many times as necessary to
obtain a very thin sheet (less than 1/8
inch).

MAKE THE FILLING: In a bowl, mix all the ingredients together with a spoon until they are well blended.

MAKE THE RAVIOLI: Spread half the pasta sheets out on a clean surface. Place teaspoons of filling at 1-inch intervals on the pasta sheets until you've used up all the filling. Make an egg wash by mixing the egg yolk with half an egg shell's worth of water. Brush the pasta sheets around the mounds of filling. Cover with the reserved sheets of pasta and press with your fingers to seal the ravioli tightly against the filling. Cut the ravioli into squares with a rolling cutter and place them on a floured tray.

MAKE THE SAUCE: Cut off and discard the bread crusts. Cut the bread into 1/2-inch cubes.

continued

If the bread is not completely stale, dry the cubes in a preheated 300°F. oven for a few minutes, until it is completely dry but still white.

In a large pot or casserole, bring the vegetable stock to a boil, then stir in the tomato sauce. When it comes back to a boil, reduce the heat to low, then add the bread, half the basil, and ¹/₄ cup of the olive oil. Season with salt and pepper and simmer, stirring frequently, until the bread has fallen apart and thickened the sauce, about 15 minutes. When you're ready to serve, stir in the black cabbage, garlic, and the rest of the basil and ¹/₄ cup more olive oil.

ASSEMBLE THE DISH: Bring a big pot of salted water to a boil and drop in the ravioli. Cook them for a minute after they float, then strain them gently by lifting them out of the pot with a slotted spoon or skimmer. Do not pour the ravioli into a colander or they will break. Arrange the ravioli on a platter. Drizzle with the remaining 3 tablespoons of olive oil, then spoon the sauce over them.

SERVES 6

Chestnut Semifreddo with Persimmon Sauce

12 egg yolks

1 cup granulated sugar

1 cup moscato wine (or any other not-
  too-sweet dessert wine)

4 cups chestnut preserves (usually
  labeled "chestnut cream")

4 cups heavy cream, whipped

Vegetable oil spray (such as Pam) to
  grease the molds

4 pounds ripe persimmons

1 cup confectioners' sugar

Juice of 2 lemons

In a metal mixing bowl set over a pan of simmering (but not boiling) water, whisk the egg yolks, granulated sugar, and wine until the mixture is frothy and thick. Remove the bowl from the water bath and keep on whisking to cool it down some. Fold in the chestnut preserves, then the whipped cream. Spray/grease 24 individual ramekins, and fill them with the mixture. Place them in the freezer until they are frozen, about 45 minutes.

Fifteen minutes before serving, dip the molds one at a time into nearly boiling water for 5 seconds, then turn them out onto individual plates. Let them thaw at room temperature.

Peel the persimmons and process them in a blender with the confectioners' sugar and lemon juice. Make pools of sauce around the semifreddo.

SERVES 24

Summer Night Seafood Extravaganza
(Serves 24)

For Italians, seafood is one of the most important parts of summer. This is as much a matter of practicality as it is of cultural taste, for great seafood is difficult to obtain in the colder months.

But seafood in the summer is also a reflection of the Tuscan communion with nature. In fact, eating fish and shellfish at this time of year is almost a form of acceptable cannibalism, since we ourselves become fish of a sort, splashing around in the water from June through August.

Personally, seafood reminds me of my time on the beaches of Tuscany as a young man. The beach is a fascinating place to study Tuscans, because if you saw us only here, you would think we were the most affected and conceited

people on the planet. Italians are proud people, who appreciate aesthetic beauty, which in the summertime means our own bodies. We train for the beach the way athletes train for the Olympics, getting into shape so we'll look good under the spotlight of the sun.

And the beach makes us wild with energy. All through Tuscany, you can see teen-agers zooming along the shore in their sportscars or on motorcycles, and dancing to whatever song happens to be popular that year.

In addition to reflecting the beach culture, seafood also reminds us of the exploratory nature of summer, because it's more exotic than any other type of food. This feast is designed to replicate the full spectrum of the aquatic world in dishes that allow many of its subjects to retain their natural shapes, and even shells, in a way that simply isn't possible with meats and poultry.

For example, the Trout Roasted Porchetta-Style (page 125), Sea Bass Cooked in Parchment Paper with Cherry Tomatoes and Leeks (page 124), and Crispy Fried Shrimp with Summer Vegetables in Sweet and Sour Vinaigrette (page 120), all present the fish or seafood whole, as if it had swum right into the oven for you.

Other traditional favorites are represented here with Calamari in Zimino (page 118) and Lobster and Cannellini Beans in Guazzetto (page 126),

dishes that adapt classic Italian formulas for modern Americans.

Lemon is a traditional accompaniment to seafood because its acidity complements almost any creature of the sea. Here, a Lemon and Mint Sorbet (page 129) is offered both to complement the preceding feast and to cleanse the palate—a mission that is supported by the mint, nature's breath freshener.

NOTE: There are six recipes here, not including dessert. Each makes enough for between six and twelve "normal" servings, but if you make them all, you'll have enough food for twenty-four people. In an everyday context, however, when serving just one or two dishes, these recipes will only serve the number of people indicated.

A Natural Setting: To emphasize the natural beauty of fish and seafood, I suggest serving it on a table dressed with natural elements, like a blanket of grass or a carved-out watermelon to hold the calamari. Be creative with this and you'll find that there's no end to what you can do.

A meal of nothing but seafood is one of the few times when white wine is actually perfect. Enjoy this feast with a Tokay or a Sauvignon Blanc.

Calamari in *Zimino*

½ cup extra virgin olive oil

1 cup chopped onion

½ cup minced carrot

½ cup chopped celery

3 cloves garlic, chopped

2½ pounds fresh calamari, cleaned,
   rinsed, bodies sliced ¼ inch wide

Salt to taste

½ teaspoon crushed hot red pepper

2 cups red wine

2½ cups diced canned tomatoes

1½ pounds fresh spinach, cleaned,
   rinsed, and spun dry

6 slices country bread, grilled

In a casserole, warm half the olive oil and sauté the chopped vegetables until they are translucent, about 5 minutes. Add the chopped garlic, mix, and sauté for 5 minutes. Stir in the calamari and add salt and red pepper. Sauté on medium-high heat for 5 minutes, then add the wine and the tomatoes. Mix and cook for another 5 minutes. Top with the spinach.

Cover the casserole, reduce the heat to very low, and do not touch for 25 minutes. Remove the lid, mix and taste for seasoning. Add the rest of the olive oil and cook for a final 10 minutes. Serve hot, with croutons of grilled country bread.

SERVES 6

Crispy Fried Shrimp with Summer Vegetables
in Sweet and Sour Vinaigrette

For the shrimp:

2 tablespoons cornstarch

1 cup ice water

1 egg

8 jumbo shrimp, head on, shells
  removed, deveined

1 quart vegetable oil, for frying

For the vegetables:

1 medium carrot, peeled and cut into
  ¼-inch dice

1 stalk celery (a tender one from
  inside), cut into ¼-inch dice

½ leek (cut lengthwise half), including
  white and light green parts, cut into
  ¼-inch dice

1 small zucchini, cut into ¼-inch dice

1 red bell pepper, seeded and cut into
  ¼-inch dice

½ teaspoon salt

2 teaspoons sugar

3 tablespoons balsamic vinegar
  (see Note)

5 tablespoons vegetable broth

3 tablespoons extra virgin olive oil

1 tablespoon chopped fresh chives

NOTE: Use only high-quality Aceto Balsamic Tradizionale di Modena.

PREPARE THE SHRIMP: In a bowl, dissolve the cornstarch in the ice water by mixing with a whisk. Add the egg and continue beating with the whisk to incorporate it. In a deep pan over medium-high heat, warm the oil until it reaches 375°F. (a drop of water will crackle and splutter). Dip the shrimp in the batter and drop them carefully into the oil. Fry until they are golden, 3 to 4 minutes, remove with a slotted spoon, and drain them on paper towels.

PREPARE THE VEGETABLES: Bring a pot of salted water to a boil. Blanch the carrot and celery for 2 minutes. Strain them and shock them by immersing them in ice water for 2 minutes, drain and pat them dry. Put them in a big bowl with the leek, zucchini, and red bell pepper. Make the vinaigrette by whisking the salt and sugar in a bowl with the balsamic vinegar and vegetable broth until they dissolve. Add the olive oil in a stream, whisking continually until the mixture is

homogenous. Pour
the vinaigrette
over the vegeta-
bles and toss
well.

Spread the veg-
etables on a
serving platter
and arrange the
fried shrimp on
top. Sprinkle
with the chives.

S E R V E S   8

Fusilli Salad
with Swordfish and Grapefruit

½ cup extra virgin olive oil

1 clove garlic, peeled

¾ pound swordfish, cut into ½-inch
   cubes

Salt and freshly ground pepper
   to taste

2 pink grapefruits

1½ pounds dry fusilli

6 scallions, cut into ½-inch slices
   (including dark green parts)

1 tablespoon dried oregano

2 tablespoons chopped fresh Italian
   parsley leaves

In a non-stick sauté pan over medium-high heat, warm 2 tablespoons of the olive oil. Add the garlic clove and the swordfish and sear the fish on all sides for a total of 3 or 4 minutes. Discard the garlic. Season the fish with salt and pepper. Remove the swordfish to a large mixing bowl.

Peel and section the grapefruits. Working over a bowl to catch the juice, use a sharp paring knife to cut away the membrane surrounding each section. Put the peeled grapefruit segments and ⅓ cup of the juice into the bowl with the swordfish.

In a large pot of boiling salted water, cook the fusilli until very al dente (slightly underdone). Strain the pasta into a colander, then spread it out in a sheet pan. Stir in 1 tablespoon of the olive oil to coat the pasta, and let it cool down to room temperature.

Add the pasta to the bowl with the swordfish and grapefruit. Add the scallions, oregano, parsley, and the remaining olive oil. Season with salt and pepper. Toss well.

SERVES 6 TO 8

Sea Bass Cooked in Parchment Paper with Cherry Tomatoes and Leeks

1 large wild sea bass (about 6 pounds), cleaned and left whole

Salt and freshly ground pepper to taste

1 sprig fresh rosemary

12 baby artichokes, trimmed of outer leaves and tops, cut vertically into quarters, and set in a bowl of water acidulated with the juice of a lemon

2 leeks, white and light green parts only, cleaned carefully and cut into ⅛-inch slices

24 cherry tomatoes, cut in half lengthwise

10 basil leaves, torn roughly by hand

1 tablespoon whole fresh marjoram leaves

1 cup Vernaccia, or another dry white wine

¼ cup extra virgin olive oil

Preheat the oven to 450°F. Place the fish on a big sheet of parchment paper or foil on a large sheet pan. Season the cavity with salt and pepper, and put the sprig of rosemary inside.

Bring a pot of water to a boil and blanch the artichokes for 1 minute, then drain them and place them all around the fish, together with the leeks and tomatoes. Sprinkle the basil and marjoram over the vegetables, then sprinkle everything with the wine and olive oil. Season with salt and pepper.

Seal the paper around the fish by rolling the edges together and pinching to crease. Bake in the preheated oven for 30 minutes. (Don't check for doneness; trust this timing to preserve the moisture and the dramatic presentation.) Bring the fish in its <u>cartoccio</u> to the table, and open it up in front of your guests.

SERVES 10 TO 12

Trout Roasted <u>Porchetta</u>-Style

¼ pound prosciutto, minced

2 ounces pancetta, minced

1 tablespoon ground fennel seeds

2 tablespoons chopped fresh rosemary

3 cloves garlic, chopped fine

4 tablespoons bread crumbs

⅓ cup white wine

1 tablespoon red wine vinegar

3 large trout, 1½ pounds each, cleaned, rinsed, and dried

Extra virgin olive oil, for brushing the fish

Preheat oven to 375°F.

In a bowl, combine all the ingredients except the fish and the olive oil. Make a 1½-inch-long diagonal slash ½ inch deep on each side of each fish. Stuff half the filling in the cuts and half in the cavities. Brush the fish with olive oil, wrap them individually in aluminum foil, and roast in the oven for 15 to 20 minutes, or until just cooked through.

SERVES 6

Summer

Lobster and Cannellini Beans in Guazzetto

For the guazzetto:

½ cup extra virgin olive oil

1 small onion, chopped

2 shallots, chopped

2 cloves garlic, sliced, plus 2 whole
    cloves

1 small Idaho potato, peeled and cut
    into ¼-inch slices

2 plum tomatoes, seeded and sliced

6 leaves fresh basil

10 leaves fresh oregano

3 cups dry cannellini beans, soaked
    overnight in water, then rinsed and
    drained

2 teaspoons salt, plus extra to taste

1 sprig fresh rosemary

Freshly ground pepper to taste

For the lobster:

4 lobsters, 1 pound each

2 plum tomatoes

2 tablespoons extra virgin olive oil

2 shallots, chopped

1 tablespoon chopped fresh oregano
    leaves

½ cup white wine

Salt and freshly ground pepper
    to taste

For the Garnish:

8 sage leaves

¼ cup extra virgin olive oil

Freshly ground black pepper to taste

MAKE THE GUAZZETTO: In a large pot over medium heat, warm half the olive oil. Add the onion, shallots, sliced garlic, potato, tomatoes, basil, and oregano. Stir well and sauté until the vegetables sweat out some of their liquid, 4 to 5 minutes. Add the drained and rinsed cannellini and mix until the beans are coated with olive oil and vegetables. Cover with water by 3 inches, season with 2 teaspoons of salt, and bring the liquid to a boil slowly over medium heat. When it reaches a slow boil, reduce the heat to low, and simmer until the beans are fork tender, about 15 minutes, adding more boiling water as necessary to keep the beans covered.

When the beans are fork tender, remove one quarter of them from the pot and set them aside. Use a hand-held immersion blender or a food processor to puree the rest, then put the reserved whole beans back in. Put the remaining

continued

olive oil in a sauté pan over medium-low heat with the whole garlic and the sprig of rosemary. When the oil sizzles around the garlic and rosemary, remove them from the pan with a fork or a slotted spoon, and pour the oil into the guazzetto. Season with salt and pepper.

MAKE THE LOBSTER: Bring a pot of water to a boil. Blanch the lobsters for 5 minutes, then remove them from the pot to cool them down. Separate the lobsters' claws from the bodies with a cleaver. When they are cool enough to handle comfortably, crack the claws open and remove the meat carefully, trying to keep each claw's meat intact. Set the claw meat aside for later.

In another pot of boiling water, blanch the tomatoes for 1 minute, then remove them and shock them in ice water for a minute. Peel the skin off, remove the seeds, and cut the tomatoes into $\frac{1}{4}$-inch dice. Cut the lobster bodies and tails in half lengthwise.

In a large, non-stick casserole over medium-high heat, warm the olive oil. Add the shallots and the lobsters, cut sides down, and cook until the meat is golden, about 3 minutes. Add the oregano and the diced tomatoes, sprinkle with the white wine, and season with salt and pepper. When the wine evaporates, about another 3 minutes, remove the lobsters from the pan. Remove the meat from the shells and put the meat back in the pan. Add the guazzetto, and simmer for 5 minutes.

To serve, pour the lobster in guazzetto into large bowls. Arrange lobster claws and sage leaves on top, drizzle with the extra virgin olive oil, and grind black pepper over all.

SERVES 12

Lemon and Mint Sorbet

3½ cups sugar

5½ cups water

4 cups freshly squeezed lemon juice

1 egg white, beaten until it forms
   stiff peaks

Fresh mint leaves, for garnish

In a saucepan over medium heat, cook the sugar and 3½ cups of the water together until the sugar has dissolved, making a light syrup, about 5 minutes. Remove the pan from the heat and let the syrup cool to room temperature.

In a bowl, mix the syrup with the lemon juice and the remaining 2 cups of water. Fold in the beaten egg white. Put the mixture into an ice cream machine and follow the manufacturer's instructions. (If you don't have an ice cream machine, you can put the bowl in the freezer and stir the mixture occasionally until it gains the consistency of sorbet.) Serve garnished with mint leaves.

SERVES 12

NOTE: To make enough for 24, prepare the recipe twice; you'll need to work in batches like this because most ice cream machines aren't big enough to hold 24 servings.

Fall

Dondato come Console a Trieffe giuffa la
quella nomina. Nè l'infor-
ffone fperle derivato
potrà fupporfi immediata-
fia, nè afcoroterfia
Governo.

fpace di doverle fcrivere
fe, e per rifparmiarle
alla prima lettera cui
da altra diverfione
Involate nuovamente
la faurò, ma non de
narla. Bramo ben
feffo, e che di
perfuafione
per Lei la fupero
ma quale ro non poffo fe non
efeguire gli ordini, dopo di averle
fubordinato gli altri, di cuore godrò
ogni volta ch' io la fappia meno
infelice.
        Colla maledetta
                div

Mysteries of the Tuscan Night

Bagni di Lucca

Fra il tonfo dei marroni	Amid the blending
e il gemito del torrente	sounds of chestnuts thudding
che uniscono i loro suoni	and the stream that moans
èsita il cuore.	the heart hesitates.

Fra il tonfo dei marroni
e il gemito del torrente
che uniscono i loro suoni
èsita il cuore.

Precoce inverno che borea
abbrividisce. M'affaccio
sul ciglio che scioglie l'albore
del giorno nel ghiaccio.

Marmi, rameggi—
          e ad uno scrollo giù
foglie a èlice, a froccia,
nel fossato.

Passa l'ultima greggia nella nebbia
del suo fiato.

—EUGENIO MONTALE

Amid the blending
sounds of chestnuts thudding
and the stream that moans
the heart hesitates.

Early winter the north wind
sets shivering. I look out
over the edge dissolving
the dawn white in ice.

Marble branches—
                    with a shake
leaves eddy, arrow down
into the ditch.

The last herd passes
in the mist of its breath.

—translated by
EAMON GRENNAN

A lot of people come to visit Tuscany in July and August, which is definitely better than not coming at all, but if you have a true sense of romance, an appreciation of history and tradition, and a soul that is attracted to the poetic, fall is the time to experience Tuscany at the height of its natural cycle.

When I think of Tuscany at this time of year, I envision an early morning fog in late September, rolling in over the hills, providing a dramatic, operatic backdrop for the farmers as they pick grapes and turn soil for the harvest, just as their parents and grandparents did before them, engaging in the strenuous, eternal work of those whose existence is intertwined with the land and the elements.

In our lives, as in nature, fall is the time for reaping what we sow. The name of this season suggests death and decay, because it implies images of leaves dropping off trees and the air turning cold against us. But I don't think of fall that way. To me the season is one of great comfort and maturity that reflects our middle years. If we have learned from our youth, and if we have planned well, we are ready for the adversity and challenges that confront us later in life, just as those of us who plan accordingly—buying the right clothes and taking proper care of our homes—are able to shield ourselves from the cold winds that blow at this time of year.

To Tuscans, fall brings to mind images of brilliant, rich landscapes highlighted by the intense ruby red of the vines after the harvest and of green-brown hills sloping down to the deep, blue sea. Sunsets at this time of year are surreal, with a pink-gold light that has to be seen to be understood. For people who wonder where the Renaissance painters got their inspiration for the colors of their palate, the answer is that they were merely capturing the intensity of Maremma, Sienna, and Florence in the fall.

This season is also a time of intense smells, such as the wet, early morning aroma of wood, mushrooms, and chestnuts, or the smoke coming off chimneys, which—no matter when I encounter it—puts me in an autumn state of mind.

But fall is something else as well. It is the time when the shadow of darkness crawls over the land earlier and earlier each day; and this, too, indicates that it is a time of maturity. For nighttime, the dark time, is when children go off to sleep and the

adults have their fun, playing in our own way into the early morning hours.

There's an extra layer of mystery in the fall, an air of the unknown and the unknowable that seems to live in the shadows of the season and tease us from time to time. It's no accident that Halloween comes in the fall, because this is the time when ghosts would be at home.

It's easy to forget about this aspect of life if you live in a big city, because the industrial world has found ways to keep itself lit at all hours, and has put up high-rises and other structures to hold the natural world at bay. But in Tuscany, where there are no barriers between man and nature, we are in touch with the entire world that moves around us.

I'm going to share with you a story that to me sums up the mysteries of the Tuscan night. In America this would be a ghost story, but it wasn't frightening when it happened. In fact, it was a perfectly comfortable time for everyone involved.

When I was in Tuscany taking pictures for this book, my friends and I began talking about the afterlife. One of them revealed to me that her mother had been a medium. We were staying in an old castle, and this woman volunteered to hold a séance. We went upstairs to the tower, and she called out to various spirits. After a while, the table started to shake, and we all felt that we were in the presence of an unseen force. It didn't speak to us, or fly around as it would in the movies. But it did move that table, and it was there. You have to believe

KODAK 5053 TMY   10   KODAK 5053 TMY   11   KODAK 5053 TMY   12

me, this was real—a real spirit called over by a friend of mine in an old home with no planning and no tricks.

Does this seem strange to you? It doesn't to me. I considered it proof of a connection to nature that seems perfectly logical. And it seems like a perfectly normal thing to have happen on an autumn night in Tuscany. I would not have had my children there for this, but, as I said, fall is a season of evenings and adults.

So, getting back to the everyday world, the safe and unstartling world, as far as entertaining is concerned, fall is the most mature season—a time for adult socializing. The weather is perfect for more serious food and for drinking great, complex wines. A fall meal is actually a form of entertain-ment, one of the few times in Tuscan life when it's appropriate to show off a little.

In fact, the purpose of a fall meal is the opposite of one in the spring or summer. In those seasons, food is just another excuse to go outside. But in the fall, food is a protest against the weather and becomes one of the most important parts of daily life.

The complexity of fall cooking is a reminder that recipes were not created in a kitchen with no windows; these recipes are as complicated and mean-ingful as our poetry, our art, and our philosophy. As you read and cook from the recipes in this chapter, keep in mind that you are, in a way, revisit-ing Italian history.

Fall

A Quintessential Fall Menu

A Quintessential Fall Menu
(Serves 4)

It's impossible to sum up the foods of fall in just a few short recipes, but here are some of my personal favorites.

The Roasted Mushroom Salad with Butternut Squash, Pearl Onions, and Chestnuts (page 139) features three very earthy ingredients, all of them browned to release their natural sugars and add an element of sweetness to the dish. I love squash and chestnuts, but this salad is the first dish on this menu because of how much mushrooms mean to me. You'll see that the first theme menu in this chapter is a truffle dinner, because truffles are my favorite delicacy in the world. But even if truffles didn't exist, the mushrooms at this time of year are truly amazing. I like to use them in all kinds of ways, grilling or sautéing them on their own, or tossing them with some pasta or in a risotto. Spend some time thinking about mushrooms whenever you're entertaining in the fall and you'll find that they're like good friends—they almost never let you down.

I include the next dish on this menu to showcase another great cold-weather food. Goat cheese and beets are a great combination at any time of year, but what makes the Goat Cheese Ravioli with Lamb Sauce (page 142) perfect for the fall is the hearty sauce that would seem out of place in the warmer months. Here, it makes the other components of the dish seem right at home in this season.

I mentioned earlier that wine is essential during the fall, and the Peposo (page 144) is a Tuscan beef and pepper stew that helps celebrate the season of the harvest with a sauce that uses great amounts of it. Don't feel that you have to use Chianti; if you have another favorite, it should work just as well. Also, be sure to save some of the cooking wine to drink with the finished dish.

Finally, to get a sense of how much a dish can literally resemble the season, take a look at the recipe instructions for the Monte Bianco (page 145), which is intended to represent a mountaintop—the perfect image with which to conclude a meal at the peak of the season, as we begin to look ahead to the colder winter months.

Roasted Mushroom Salad
with Butternut Squash, Pearl Onions and Chestnuts

2 pounds mixed wild mushrooms, such
    as shiitake, oyster, and chanterelle,
    tough stems removed, mushrooms
    quickly washed and dried
6 tablespoons extra virgin olive oil
4 teaspoons whole thyme leaves
4 tablespoons whole fresh rosemary
    leaves
4 bay leaves
Salt and freshly ground pepper
    to taste
3 cups ½-inch cubes of peeled and
    seeded butternut squash
20 pearl onions, peeled and blanched
    for 1 minute
20 chestnuts, boiled and peeled (frozen
    peeled chestnuts are easier to use)
1 teaspoon balsamic vinegar
¼ pound cleaned and dried mesclun
    salad greens

Preheat the oven to 400°F.

Toss the mushrooms in a roasting pan
with 1½ tablespoons of the olive oil,
2 teaspoons of the thyme, 1 tablespoon
of the rosemary, 1 bay leaf, and salt
and pepper. Roast in the preheated
oven for 20 minutes, mixing the mushrooms around twice to ensure even
cooking.

In a roasting pan, toss the squash and
the onions with 2 tablespoons of the
remaining olive oil, 1 teaspoon of the
remaining rosemary, the remaining
thyme, 2 bay leaves, and salt and pepper. Roast in the preheated oven for
20 minutes, mixing the vegetables
around twice to ensure even cooking.
The squash should be firm and the
onions slightly browned. Reduce the
oven temperature to 300°.

In a pot of boiling water, blanch and
drain the chestnuts. Then toss them in
a roasting pan with ½ tablespoon of
the remaining olive oil and the
remaining rosemary and bay leaf. Roast
them in the preheated oven for 20 minutes, until the chestnuts are deep
gold in color. Mix the chestnuts with
the squash, onions, and mushrooms.
Season with salt and pepper.

In a large salad bowl, mix the vinegar
with a pinch of salt, then add the
remaining 2 tablespoons of olive oil,
beating well. Add the greens and toss
well. Arrange the salad in the middle
of 4 plates. Spoon the roasted vegetable mixture over the salad.

Serves 4

Fall

139

Goat Cheese Ravioli with Lamb Sauce

For the pasta:

8 cups (2 pounds) flour
10 whole eggs

For the filling:

1½ pounds fresh goat cheese
6 ounces mascarpone cheese
2 egg yolks
⅓ cup freshly grated Parmesan cheese
¼ cup fresh, fine bread crumbs
⅔ cup finely diced cooked beets
Grated zest of ½ lemon
½ teaspoon ground cloves
½ teaspoon ground juniper berries
Salt and freshly ground pepper
   to taste

For the lamb sauce:

4 tablespoons olive oil
2 pounds lamb stewing meat, cut into
   ½-inch cubes
Salt and freshly ground pepper
   to taste
⅔ cup finely diced celery
⅔ cup finely diced carrot
⅔ cup finely diced onion

1½ cups red wine vinegar
1 bouquet garni (1 clove garlic, 1 sprig
   fresh rosemary, 3 sprigs fresh
   thyme, 2 bay leaves, 4 whole cloves,
   1 teaspoon whole black
   peppercorns, 1 tablespoon whole
   juniper berries, 1 tablespoon fennel
   seeds, all tied in cheesecloth)
Grated zest of 1 lemon
2 cups red wine
1 cup veal or chicken stock or broth
1 teaspoon ground cloves
1 teaspoon ground juniper berries

MAKE THE PASTA: On a clean, smooth surface, mound the flour and make a well in the center. Add the eggs and mix the flour into the center with a fork, a little at a time, until all the flour has been absorbed. Knead with your hands until the dough is elastic. Pass the dough through the pasta machine as many times as necessary to obtain a very thin sheet (less than ⅛ inch).

MAKE THE FILLING: In a bowl, combine all the ingredients until the mixture is homogenous.

MAKE THE RAVIOLI: Lay the pasta sheet out so that at least half of it is flat. Place a teaspoon of filling at 1½-inch intervals over half of the sheet. A pastry bag is the easiest way to do this, but you can use a spoon and your fingers, too. Fold the other half of the sheet over the half with the filling, and press with your fingers all over, to make sure there is no air trapped between the sheets. Using a pastry cutter, cut the sheets into 2-inch squares or rounds, with the filling centered in each.

MAKE THE SAUCE: In a wide, heavy casserole with a snug-fitting lid over high heat, warm 2 tablespoons of the olive oil. Add the lamb, season with salt and pepper, and sear on all sides, turning about every other minute until all sides of each cube are browned, about 6 minutes total. Remove the lamb to a colander to drain the juices. Clean the pan, add the remaining olive oil, and warm it over low heat. Add the celery, carrot, and onion, and cook until the onion is soft, about 3 minutes, stirring occasionally. Add the lamb, turn the heat up to medium, and cook until the meat is brown. Add the vinegar to deglaze the pan, scraping up all the brown bits on the bottom. When the vinegar evaporates, about 2 minutes, add the bouquet garni, the lemon zest, and the wine.

When the alcohol has evaporated (it takes about 10 minutes—you can tell because it stops smelling acidic), add the stock and season with salt and pepper. Simmer, covered, for 45 minutes, until the lamb is very tender. Add the ground cloves and ground juniper berries.

ASSEMBLE: In a pot of boiling salted water, cook the ravioli until they float, about 5 minutes. Remove the ravioli with a slotted spoon to the pan with the sauce. Cook together for 2 minutes, then serve.

MAKES 70 TO 80 RAVIOLI, OR ABOUT 8 MAIN COURSE SERVINGS

NOTE: Extra uncooked ravioli may be frozen in the following manner: Allow them to freeze on a sheet pan placed in the freezer. After they have hardened, place them in a bag for easy storage. The sauce may also be frozen separately.

Peposo

Tuscan Beef and Pepper Stew

⅓ cup extra virgin olive oil

2 pounds beef stewing meat, cut into
   1-inch cubes

⅔ cup finely chopped carrot

⅔ cup finely chopped onion

⅔ cup finely chopped celery

Salt to taste

2 cups red wine, preferably Chianti

3 cups chicken stock, broth, or bouillon

⅓ cup Basic Tomato Sauce
   (page 93)

1 pound butternut squash, peeled,
   seeded, and cut into 1-inch cubes
   (about 3 cups)

4 tablespoons crushed black
   peppercorns

In a heavy casserole over high heat, warm half of the olive oil. Add the beef and sear it on all sides, turning every other minute until all sides of the cubes are browned, about 6 minutes total. Remove the beef and set it aside.

Reduce the heat to low, and add the remaining olive oil to the casserole. Add the carrot, onion, celery, and salt. Mix the seared beef in the pan with the vegetables and cook together for 2 minutes. Add the red wine and scrape the browned bits from the bottom of the pan. Continue cooking until there is almost no liquid left in the pan, about 4 minutes. Add the stock and the tomato sauce and simmer for 15 minutes. Add half the squash and all the peppercorns. Add water if there is not enough liquid to cover the solids. Bring to a boil, reduce the heat to low, cover, and simmer for an hour, stirring occasionally. When the meat is very tender, add the rest of the squash. Cook for another 20 minutes, covered, until the cubes of squash are tender. Add salt if necessary.

Terrific served over polenta (see recipe, page 101).

SERVES 4

Monte Bianco

2 pounds whole fresh chestnuts, boiled
 and peeled of shells and inner skins;
 or 1½ pounds peeled frozen
 chestnuts
1 quart whole milk
1 vanilla bean, split open lengthwise
4 cups sugar (see recipe)
2 cups heavy cream

In a heavy pot or casserole, combine the peeled chestnuts, milk, and vanilla bean. Simmer over medium heat, covered, until the milk has been absorbed, about 45 minutes. Mash the chestnuts by passing them through a sieve or by using a potato ricer or masher. Weigh the mixture, and add half its weight in sugar. Put the mixture back in the casserole. Cook on low heat until the mixture reaches the consistency of mashed potatoes, about 20 minutes. Mash again to ensure an even texture, and turn the mixture out onto a round serving platter, mounding it into the shape of an Alp.

In a bowl, beat the remaining sugar into the heavy cream until the cream forms peaks. Top the mountain with the whipped cream as if it were snow. Keep refrigerated until serving time.

SERVES 4 TO 6

Fall's First Truffle Dinner
(Serves 6)

If you could speak to Nature and ask of it, "What is your idea of a wonderful perfume, a perfume that you, yourself, could wear and be enhanced by?" Nature's answer would be a simple one: "Truffles."

Truffles are as mysterious and beguiling as the fall itself. How many of us even know what a truffle is exactly? It's not a mushroom, really, but it does grow out of the earth, a naturally precious delicacy. Like mushrooms, truffles should not be washed clean, but rather brushed delicately to relieve them of any dirt or grime.

The power of a truffle is as irrepressible as the fall weather itself, so much so that after you store one in rice, the rice becomes impregnated with its aroma.

My favorite way to eat truffles is with perfectly cooked, sunny-side-up eggs and some freshly cracked black pepper. But, however you like them, truffles

should always be enjoyed in the simplest form possible. You want to smell the saltiness, iron, and chestnuts—all in perfect balance.

This chapter features some memorable ways to enjoy truffles. But you should definitely experiment by using them in other recipes. It's almost impossible to go wrong.

There's actually a mushroom rarer than the truffle—the ovuli—which looks like an egg. I first tasted one in my twenties, and it was love at first sight. Like most brilliant foods, it has a very short season that runs from September to early October. It also has a very limited use, because the ovuli is only served in salad, which is an amazing reminder of the talent of Mother Nature, because absolutely no cooking is required. It's almost impossible to get an ovuli here in the United States, but if you have a chance to experience one in Tuscany, don't hesitate even for a second.

Fall

147

Butternut Squash Soup
with Amaretti Cookies and Black Truffle

1 butternut squash, about 3 pounds

4 tablespoons extra virgin olive oil

1 large Spanish onion, chopped

Salt and freshly ground pepper
  to taste

12 amaretti cookies, crumbled
  to a powder

1 teaspoon grated nutmeg

½ cup freshly grated Parmesan cheese

1 ounce black truffle, shaved, for
  garnish

Peel the squash with a vegetable peeler or paring knife. Cut it into quarters. Remove and discard the seeds. Chop the flesh into ½-inch dice.

In a soup pot over medium heat, warm the olive oil. Add the onion and sauté until it's translucent, about 5 minutes. Add the squash, season with salt and pepper, and mix well. After 5 minutes, add water to cover the squash and cook until the squash is soft, about 7 minutes.

Puree the soup in a blender or food processor and pour back into the pot, on very low heat. Add three quarters of the powdered cookies and the nutmeg. Season with additional salt and pepper if necessary. Cook 5 minutes more. Remove the pot from the heat, add the cheese, and pour the soup into bowls. Garnish each serving with freshly shaved black truffle, and sprinkle with the remaining cookies.

SERVES 4 TO 6

Cardoon Risotto
with Parmesan Cheese and White Truffle

For the broth:

1 onion, peeled and halved

2 carrots, peeled

2 stalks celery

2 leeks, white and light green parts
   only, halved lengthwise

10 cups water

For the risotto:

3 pounds fresh cardoons

Juice of 1 lemon

1 tablespoon flour

1 cup cold water

⅓ cup extra virgin olive oil

⅓ cup finely chopped onion

1¾ cups Italian rice (Vialone Nano,
   Carnaroli, or arborio)

½ cup dry white wine

3 tablespoons unsalted butter

½ cup freshly grated Parmesan cheese

Salt and freshly ground pepper
   to taste

½ ounce white truffle, shaved

MAKE THE BROTH: Put all of the ingredients in a large pot. If the water doesn't cover the solids, add more. Cover the pot and bring the broth to a boil over high heat. Reduce the heat to low and simmer, partially covered, for an hour. Remove the solids by pouring the broth through a strainer. Return the broth to the pot and keep it at a simmer to use in the risotto.

MAKE THE RISOTTO: Remove and discard the tough outer ribs of the cardoons. Remove the strings from the remaining ribs with a vegetable peeler. Cut the ribs into 2-inch pieces and put them into a bowl with water and the lemon juice. Bring a large pot of salted water to a boil. Mix the flour with the cold water until it has dissolved and add it to the pot. Strain the cardoons and add them to the boiling water. Cook them for about 30 minutes or until tender, then drain them in a colander. Cut them into ½-inch slices. Put 2 cups of sliced cardoons (reserve the rest) in a blender or processor with 1 cup of the vegetable broth. Blend or pulse until they make a puree.

In a large, heavy casserole over medium heat, warm half the olive oil. Add the onion and sauté until it is translucent, about 5 minutes. Stir in the rice with a wooden spoon until it is hot and completely coated with oil and onion. Stir in the wine. When the liquid evaporates, stir in the reserved sliced cardoons. Add a ladle

about 12 minutes. (You will probably use 6 cups total.) Then continue with the ladle-at-a-time process, only using the cardoon puree. When the mixture gets too thick to cook without sticking, use the broth again. You may not need all of the cardoon puree or all of the broth; conversely, you may need to add extra hot water, depending on the shape of your pan, the heat, the rice, etc. The risotto should be done after it cooks for a total of 18 to 20 minutes. Each grain will be soft on the outside, with a slightly chewy center.

Remove the risotto from the heat and beat in the butter, the remaining olive oil, and the grated Parmesan. Stir vigorously to make the risotto creamy and all'onda (wavy). If it seems too dry, adjust the texture

of simmering broth to the rice and stir. When the liquid has been absorbed, add another ladle of broth. Continue in this way, letting the liquid absorb before adding another ladleful, and stirring frequently, for

with a bit more broth. Season with salt and pepper, spoon onto individual plates, and top each serving with shaved truffle. Serve immediately.

SERVES 6

Roasted Wild Pheasant with Brussels Sprouts, Pomegranates, and Shaved White Truffle

1 whole pheasant, about 3½ pounds

1 tablespoon chopped fresh rosemary

1 tablespoon chopped fresh thyme

Salt and freshly ground pepper to taste

4 ounces pancetta, thinly sliced

⅓ cup extra virgin olive oil

1 cup dry marsala

1 cup chicken stock

¾ pound fresh chanterelle mushrooms (substitute shiitake if chanterelles are unavailable)

¾ pound Brussels sprouts, outer leaves trimmed off, stems marked with an X using a knife, blanched for 3 minutes in boiling salted water

2 ounces fresh white truffle, shaved

Rinse the bird thoroughly and pat it dry. Put the chopped rosemary and sage in the cavity, and season the inside well with salt and pepper. Cover the pheasant with the pancetta, and tie it like a ham, with several lengths of string circling it crosswise, and one circling it lengthwise.

In a large, heavy casserole over medium-high heat, warm half the olive oil. Put the pheasant in the hot oil and sear it on all sides until golden brown all over. Cover the pan with a tight-fitting lid, reduce the heat to medium, and continue cooking for 15 minutes. Sprinkle the marsala over the pheasant, cover again, and cook until the liquid has reduced by half, about 5 minutes. Add the chicken stock and continue cooking.

Clean the mushrooms with a damp towel and cut them into lengthwise quarters. In a large heavy skillet over high heat, warm the remaining olive oil. Add the mushrooms and sauté them for 6 or 7 minutes to remove the excess water. Add the mushrooms and the blanched Brussels sprouts to the pheasant, adjust the seasoning, put the cover back on, and cook for 20 minutes more, or until the meat is tender and the juice runs clear when pierced with a sharp knife in the thickest part of the thigh.

Remove the pheasant to a platter. Surround the bird with the mushrooms and Brussels sprouts. Serve the sauce on the side. Shave some truffle on each serving.

SERVES 6

Black Truffle Sabayon

3½ ounces fresh black truffle
   (preferably Italian, from Norcia)
6 eggs
6 tablespoons sugar
4 tablespoons marsala
12 small biscotti or other dry cookies

"TRUFFLE-IZE" THE EGGS: Place the truffles and the eggs together in a tightly closed glass or plastic container or plastic bag. Refrigerate for 24 hours.

Separate the "truffle-ized" eggs. In a metal mixing bowl, combine the yolks with the sugar and marsala. Beat with a whisk until well blended. Set up a double boiler by putting a saucepan on low heat with an inch or two of water. Place the bowl on the open saucepan so that the steam rising from the water warms the bowl. Beat continually with the whisk for 10 minutes, or until the mixture has reached a custardlike texture.

Serve the sabayon hot, in individual bowls, with the cookies on the side.

SERVES 6 TO 8

A Tuscan Thanksgiving Dinner
(Serves 12)

Thanksgiving is an American holiday, but I love celebrating it because it's a chance to say "thank you" to Nature for everything we have, which is actually a very Tuscan concept. When November arrives, I apply my Tuscan sense of community and belonging and participate in the holiday along with my friends and my American family.

It's also very Tuscan to somehow work a great meal into an evening that's about gratitude, which seems funny to me somehow because you're basically saying "thank you" with your mouth full of food!

But there are some things that just don't work for me about Thanksgiving—and the biggest problem I have is with that big bird. To be perfectly honest, I prefer a stuffed goose. To me, the difference between a goose and a turkey is like the difference between a Ferrari and a Fiat—there's simply no comparison. This has to do with the size: For great flavor, and for the proper proportion of meat to stuffing, you need a bird that weighs only a few pounds.

For all of you turkey-lovers, please know that it's nothing personal between me and the turkey. Turkeys have never done anything to me, and I've never done anything to them. In fact, I may be the greatest lover of turkey in America because I don't want to kill and eat them . . . ever!

(In addition to goose, another good Thanksgiving alternative is capon, which may be more familiar to those of you used to the one that gobbles.)

Because this is the central holiday of the season in America, I've tried to use all the key fall ingredients here: pears—Pear, Pecorino, and Speck Tart (page 157); Brussels sprouts—Brussels Sprouts with Oranges (page 167); farro—Farro, Swiss Chard, and Butternut Squash Soup (page 159); and squash—(in the preceding soup, and in Butternut Squash Cappellacci with Brown Butter and Nutmeg (page 160).

This is a very filling meal, so I suggest you keep dessert simple with either a Caramel Rice Cake with Amaretto (page 169) or Spiced Poached Pears with Vin Santo Sabayon (page 170).

Try to put some of these Tuscan dishes in your next holiday dinner. I promise: You'll have something else to be thankful for.

Fall

Pear, Pecorino, and Speck Tart

10 ounces pecorino Toscano sheep's
    milk cheese, diced (a young
    manchego could substitute)
2 eggs
2 ounces fresh goat cheese
2 tablespoons heavy cream
3 teaspoons fresh thyme leaves
Salt and freshly ground pepper
    to taste
12 ounces puff pastry
3 good pears, not too soft
5 ounces smoked prosciutto (speck),
    thinly sliced
3 tablespoons shelled pistachios

In a food processor, pulse the
pecorino with the eggs, goat cheese,
cream, thyme, and salt and pepper
until well mixed, but not pureed.
Grease an 11-inch tart pan with butter. Preheat the oven to 300°F.

Roll out the puff pastry into a circle
1/4 inch thick, and arrange it to cover
the bottom and sides of the pan. Cover
the dough with foil and weigh it down
with pie weights or a couple of hand-
fuls of dry beans. Bake in the
preheated oven for 10 minutes.

While the crust is baking, halve and
core the pears and cut each one
lengthwise into 8 wedges. When the
crust is parbaked, remove the foil and
pour half the cheese-egg mixture into
the pie shell. Drape the prosciutto
slices over the cheese-egg mixture and
arrange the pears on top. Finish by
pouring the remaining cheese-egg mixture over the pears. Bake at 300° for
another 20 minutes, or until the top
is golden.

SERVES 10 TO 12

Savory Custard with Herbs and Black Truffle

3⅓ cups heavy cream

1 cup whole milk

½ cup finely chopped onion

6 tablespoons freshly grated Parmesan
   cheese

1 tablespoon finely chopped sage
   leaves

2 tablespoons chopped fresh rosemary

1 tablespoon chopped fresh thyme

1 teaspoon grated nutmeg

Salt and freshly ground pepper
   to taste

6 eggs, beaten

10 ounces black truffles, shaved

Preheat the oven to 350°F. Butter 12
individual ramekins.

In a large mixing bowl, combine the
cream, milk, onion, cheese, herbs,
nutmeg, and salt and pepper. Add the
beaten eggs and mix well. Pour the
mixture into the individual ramekins.

Make a water bath by placing the
ramekins in a roasting pan filled with
½ inch of water. Bake in the preheated oven until the custards are
golden brown on top and firm, 20 to 25
minutes. Serve by turning them out,
preferably onto a grape leaf. For a
real treat, sprinkle some fresh truffle over each serving while still
warm.

Serves 12

Farro, Swiss Chard, and Butternut Squash Soup

½ cup extra virgin olive oil, plus more
   to drizzle over each serving

1 cup chopped onion

4 Idaho potatoes, peeled and cut into
   ½-inch cubes

2 pounds butternut squash, peeled and
   seeded, cut into ½-inch cubes

Salt and freshly ground pepper
   to taste

3 pounds Swiss chard, trimmed of
   tough stalks, rinsed well, and cut into
   ½-inch slices

8 cups vegetable stock or water

3 cups farro (see page 111)

In a soup pot over medium heat, warm the olive oil. Add the onion and sauté until translucent, about 5 minutes. Add the potatoes and the squash, season with salt and pepper, and stir to coat with the oil and onion. Add the chard, mix well again, and then add the stock or water. Raise the heat to high. When the chard has wilted, about 2 minutes, add the farro, and if needed, more liquid to cover the ingredients. When the soup comes to a boil, reduce the heat to low and simmer, partially covered, until the ingredients are cooked, about 30 minutes. If the farro takes longer to cook, keep on cooking, making sure to add more liquid if necessary to keep the ingredients covered. Season with salt and pepper. Drizzle more extra virgin olive oil over each serving.

SERVES 12

Butternut Squash Cappellacci with Brown Butter and Nutmeg

For the pasta:

5¼ cups flour
6 eggs plus 1 egg yolk

For the filling:

5 pounds butternut squash
2 cups grated Parmesan cheese
2 cups finely crumbled amaretti cookies
Grated zest of 1 lemon
2 egg yolks
2 tablespoons bread crumbs
2 teaspoons grated nutmeg
Salt and freshly ground pepper
   to taste

For the sauce:

8 tablespoons unsalted butter
15 leaves fresh sage
8 tablespoons freshly grated
   Parmesan cheese

MAKE THE DOUGH: On a clean, smooth surface, mound the flour and make a well in the center. Add the whole eggs and mix the flour into the center with a fork a little at a time until all the flour has been absorbed. Knead with your hands until the dough has a smooth and even consistency. Pass the dough through the pasta machine as many times as necessary to obtain a very thin sheet (less than ⅛ inch).

MAKE THE FILLING: Preheat the oven to 325°F. Peel the squash, then cut it in half and discard the seeds. Cut the squash into 2-inch chunks, place them on a baking sheet, and cover them with foil. Bake in the preheated oven for an hour, or until they're tender and dry. Let the squash cool, then mash it until smooth (you can do this with a potato masher, a ricer, or a food processor), and squeeze out all the excess water by placing the puree in the center of a clean kitchen towel, picking up the corners, and twisting them together over the sink. Combine the drained squash with the other filling ingredients in a mixing bowl.

To assemble, cut the pasta sheet into 3-inch squares. Make an egg wash by mixing the egg yolk with half an eggshell full of water. Brush the pasta squares with the egg wash. Place 2 teaspoons of the filling onto each square. Fold the squares into triangles by bringing two opposite corners together. Seal the triangles by pressing down on the edges with your fingers. Put your index finger at the center of the folded edge of the triangle. Fold the corners down around the index finger with your other hand, pinching them together between thumb and index finger.

Cook the cappellacci in plenty of boiling salted water until they float. Drain carefully by lifting the cappellacci out of the water with a slotted spoon or skimmer—do not pour them into a colander, or they will fall apart.

MAKE THE SAUCE: In a small pan over low heat, melt the butter. Add the sage, and let it cook until the butter is golden brown, about 2 minutes.

Arrange the cappellacci on warm plates, sprinkle with the grated Parmesan, and drizzle the butter and sage over them.

SERVES 6

Goose with Vineyard Stuffing

Vegetable oil cooking spray

1 quince, peeled, cored, and cut into
    1-inch dice

1 pear, peeled, cored, and cut into
    1-inch dice

2 tablespoons dark brown sugar

4 ounces ground chicken breast

4 ounces ground pork

4 ounces loose sausage meat

1 cup freshly grated Parmesan cheese

1 cup bread crumbs

1 egg

2 tablespoons salt

Freshly ground black pepper to taste

½ teaspoon grated nutmeg

½ cup dried sour cherries, soaked in
    warm water for 30 minutes to plump,
    then drained

½ pound red grapes, preferably
    seedless

Seeds of 1 pomegranate

1 goose, approximately 6 pounds

4 tablespoons butter

½ cup extra virgin olive oil

2 cups white wine

1 cup chicken stock

Preheat the oven to 200°F. Line a sheet pan with parchment paper. Spray the parchment paper with vegetable oil spray. Place the quince and the pear in a single layer on the parchment paper and sprinkle the brown sugar on top. Bake in the preheated oven until caramelized, about 45 minutes.

Meanwhile, in a bowl, combine the ground chicken and pork with the loose sausage meat, Parmesan, bread crumbs, egg, ½ tablespoon of the salt, pepper, and nutmeg. When the mixture is amalgamated, add the quince and pear, along with the dried cherries, grapes, and pomegranate seeds.

Turn the oven up to 375°. Spoon the stuffing loosely into the main cavity of the goose (if there's extra, you can cook it in a buttered ovenproof dish). Rub the butter all over the goose, then season it with 1½ tablespoons of the salt. Tuck the wing tips under the goose, and tie the legs together. Pour the olive oil into a roasting pan and place the goose in it, breast side up. Roast in the top third of the preheated oven until the goose begins to turn brown, about 30

minutes. Reduce the temperature to 325°, pour the white wine over the goose, and cover it loosely with foil. Continue roasting, adding the stock when the wine has evaporated, and basting every 20 minutes, for 2 hours, or until an instant-read thermometer placed in the thickest part of the thigh registers 180°.

Transfer the goose to a carving board with channels to hold the juice, cover it again with foil, and let it rest for a good 20 minutes before carving.

SERVES 12

Fall

Brussels Sprouts with Oranges

1 pound Brussels sprouts, outer leaves
   removed
4 tablespoons olive oil
½ cup finely chopped onion
1 pound butternut squash, peeled,
   seeded, and cut into ½-inch cubes
1 cup vegetable stock
Salt and freshly ground pepper
   to taste
¾ cup freshly squeezed orange juice
12 chestnuts, peeled (see Note)

*NOTE: The best way to peel chestnuts
is to take one in the palm of your
hand, concave side down. Make an
incision with a paring knife, and peel
from the incision in all directions.*

Bring a pot of salted water to a
boil. Blanch the Brussels sprouts for
3 minutes, strain them, and spread
them out to cool at room temperature.
In a large, heavy saucepan over medium
heat, warm the oil. Add the onion and
cook until it turns translucent, about
5 minutes. Stir in the squash and cook
for 2 minutes more. Add half the vegetable stock and season with salt and
pepper. After 5 minutes, add the Brussels sprouts and the orange juice, and
cook for another 20 minutes. Add the
chestnuts. If there is not enough liquid in the pan to prevent scorching,
add more vegetable stock. Continue
cooking until the vegetables are quite
tender but still firm enough to eat
with a fork, and the sauce is a little
caramelized, about 15 minutes more.

SERVES 12

Mashed Potatoes and Leeks

8 tablespoons unsalted butter

2 leeks, trimmed of dark green parts,
    rinsed well, and finely diced

½ cup vegetable stock

Salt and freshly ground pepper
    to taste

2 pounds Idaho potatoes

½ cup hot milk

1 cup freshly grated Parmesan cheese

In a wide saucepan over very low heat, melt 1 tablespoon of the butter. Add the leeks and braise them, covered, until they are very soft, about 30 minutes; add some of the vegetable stock if they stick to the bottom of the pan. Season with salt and pepper.

Bring a pot of lightly salted water to a boil. Boil the potatoes until they are fork tender, about 12 to 15 minutes, then drain and peel them. Pass the potatoes through a ricer or a food mill, and then put them back into the pot (now dry) on a very low flame. Add the rest of the butter, the milk, and the Parmesan, and beat vigorously with a wooden spoon to blend. Season with salt and pepper, then stir in the braised leeks.

SERVES 12

Caramel Rice Cake with Amaretto

4 cups whole milk

1 vanilla bean, split open lengthwise

Zest of ½ lemon, whole or in big pieces

¾ cup Italian rice (arborio, Vialone
  Nano, or Carnaroli)

1 cup chopped toasted almonds

1 cup diced candied lemon peel

10 eggs

3½ cups sugar

¼ cup water

½ cup Amaretto di Saronno liqueur

In a large saucepan, bring the milk to a boil with the vanilla bean and the lemon zest. When the milk reaches a boil, stir in the rice. When it comes back to a boil, reduce the heat to low and simmer, uncovered, until the rice is soft, about 30 minutes. Remove the pan from the heat and let the milk cool down to room temperature. Remove and discard the vanilla bean and lemon zest, and add the almonds and candied lemon peel.

In a bowl, mix the eggs with 2½ cups of the sugar, making sure not to beat too vigorously—you don't want the eggs to foam. When the sugar has dissolved, add the egg mixture to the rice, mixing thoroughly.

Preheat the oven to 325°F.

In a skillet over medium heat, make the caramel by heating the remaining cup of sugar with the water until the sugar dissolves and the liquid becomes the color of caramel, 3 to 4 minutes. Pour the caramel evenly into a 2-quart non-stick savarin mold. Add the rice to the savarin mold. Bake in the preheated oven for 30 minutes. Reduce the heat to 300° and bake for another 10 minutes, or until a toothpick inserted in the center comes out clean. Let the cake cool for 15 minutes, then turn it out onto a platter and pour the amaretto over it.

Serves 12

Dried Sour Cherry Compote

4 cups dried sour cherries, soaked for
   30 minutes in warm water

Julienned zest of 1 orange

Juice of 1 orange

2 tablespoons sugar

1 cup red wine

2 whole cloves

1-inch piece of cinnamon stick

In a small casserole over high heat, place all the ingredients together.

When the liquid comes to a boil, reduce the heat to low, cover, and simmer until the texture is creamy, about 30 minutes.

SERVES 12

NOTE: This may be used as a relish with the goose; essentially, it's an alternative to cranberries.

Spiced Poached Pears with Vin Santo Sabayon

For the pears:

2 quarts water

1 pound sugar

Grated zest of ½ lemon

3-inch piece of cinnamon stick

2 whole cloves

2 bay leaves

12 slightly underripe Bartlett pears,
   peeled but left whole

For the sabayon:

10 egg yolks

⅞ cup sugar

½ teaspoon ground cinnamon

½ cup Vin Santo

POACH THE PEARS: In a large pot, bring the water to a boil with the sugar, lemon zest, spices, and bay leaves. Cook until the liquid is reduced to a medium syrup, about 20 minutes. Add the pears and simmer them over low heat until tender but still firm, another 7 to 8 minutes. Let them cool in the cooking liquid.

MAKE THE SABAYON: Warm a shallow bowl by placing it over a pot of simmering water. Beat the eggs, sugar, and cinnamon in the bowl with a wire whisk. Add the Vin Santo, whipping continually until the mixture is creamy.

On a platter, arrange the pears as you wish, topping each one with a spoonful of sabayon.

S E R V E S   1 2

A Dinner Date for Two Prepared by Him
(Serves 2)

Here in the United States, when people find out that a man can cook, it's as if they've learned that he can fly, or has some other supernatural power. So I almost feel sorry for myself and other Tuscan men, because in Tuscany, it is nothing special for a man to be able to cook. It's actually as common as being able to walk. In fact, if a man can't cook in Tuscany, he has something to be ashamed of.

But there are many different types of cooking. There's the kind of cooking we do for ourselves for daily sustenance. There's the kind of cooking we do for groups of people, as we do for the holidays. And then there's the kind of cooking we do in the name of romance, creating a meal meant to be enjoyed by candlelight.

This is such a meal, a beautiful little feast that is loaded with bold, passionate flavors.

It begins with a stunning Black Pepper-Crusted Swordfish Carpaccio (page 174), which has a pungent, slightly spicy flavor from the pepper that is cooled by a lentil salad. The Garganelli with Radicchio, Pancetta, and Balsamic Vinegar (page 176) is also quite visually arresting—a hearty, substantial pasta with autumnal colors and flavors.

Striped Bass in "Crazy Water" (page 179) is my version of a Neopolitan classic that finds a fish cooked in sea water. Here, herbs are mixed into the water to make the flavor even more powerful.

Finally, the Parmesan Gelato (page 180) is impressive. It's an alternative to a cheese course that is matched with the classic seasonal flavors of pears and walnuts. This is a very clever way to end a meal without its being too heavy—a good thing where romance is concerned! (And you'll find that the Semifreddo with Torrone and Orange Sauce on page 183 is a lighter-than-usual dessert as well.)

How good is this meal? If you prepare it for someone you are interested in, and she still demonstrates some doubt about you, you should forget about her and move on.

Black Pepper-Crusted Swordfish Carpaccio

For the carpaccio:

½ pound center-cut swordfish fillet
¼ cup crushed black pepper
1½ tablespoons extra virgin olive oil

For the lentil salad:

1 cup green lentils
1 small carrot, peeled
1 small onion, peeled

1 small stalk celery, rinsed
¾ teaspoon salt
½ red bell pepper, diced to same size
  as lentils
½ yellow bell pepper, diced to same
  size as lentils
1 scallion, sliced ⅛ inch thick
1 tablespoon red wine vinegar
3 tablespoons extra virgin olive oil

PREPARE THE CARPACCIO: Roll the swordfish in the black pepper to fully coat it. Wrap the fish in plastic wrap and place it in the refrigerator until it is firm, about 1 hour, so that you can slice it very thin (ideally with a mandoline or slicing machine).

PREPARE THE SALAD: Rinse the lentils, put them in a pot and cover them completely with cold water. Add the carrot, onion, and celery, 1/2 teaspoon of the salt, and bring to a boil. Lower the flame and simmer for about 25 to 30 minutes, until the lentils are cooked but still firm. Strain the lentils, but save some cooking water to keep them juicy.

Allow the lentils and vegetables to cool to room temperature, remove and discard the carrot, onion, and celery, then place the lentils in a bowl with the diced peppers and the scallion. Dissolve 1/4 teaspoon salt with the vinegar, whisking and adding the olive oil until emulsified. Toss the lentils with the dressing, mixing thoroughly.

Slice the carpaccio about 1/8 inch thick and arrange it on individual plates. Place the lentil salad in the center. Drizzle with the extra virgin olive oil.

SERVES 2

NOTE: If you do not use all the carpaccio, wrap the leftover piece in plastic wrap and place it in the freezer where it will last for a long time.

Garganelli with Radicchio, Pancetta, and Balsamic Vinegar

3 cups flour

2 eggs, plus 3 egg yolks

4 tablespoons olive oil

4 shallots, chopped

3 ounces pancetta, diced

2 cups cleaned, ½-inch slices radicchio

4 tablespoons unsalted butter

4 tablespoons freshly grated Parmesan cheese

4 teaspoons very good aged balsamic vinegar (see Note)

NOTE: Use only high-quality Aceto Balsamico Tradizionale di Modena.

MAKE THE DOUGH: On a clean, smooth surface, mound the flour and make a well in the center. Add the eggs and yolks and mix the flour into the center with a fork a little at a time until all the flour has been absorbed. Knead with your hands until the dough has a smooth and even consistency. Pass the dough through the pasta machine as many times as necessary to obtain a very thin sheet (less than $1/8$ inch). Cut the pasta into 2-inch squares. Form the squares into garganelli by rolling them corner to corner, one at a time, onto a garganelli tool or a pencil. If you're using a pencil, you can mark the garganelli with ridges with a wooden butter stamper.

Put a large pot of salted water up to boil for the pasta. In a large sauté pan over medium-high heat, warm the olive oil. Add the shallots and pancetta and cook until the shallots are golden, about 5 minutes. Add the radicchio and stir-fry until it is wilted. Remove from the heat. Cook the pasta for 2 or 3 minutes, until it is al dente, then drain it and add it to the sauce in the pan, tossing everything together over medium heat. Toss with the butter and the Parmesan. Sprinkle with the balsamic vinegar and serve.

SERVES 2

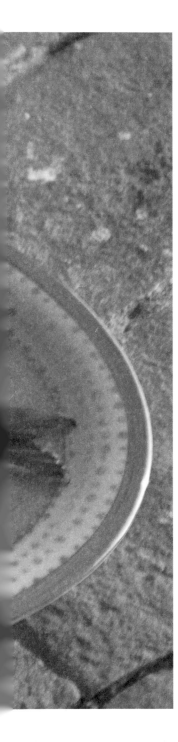

Striped Bass in "Crazy Water"

2 striped bass
   (snappers may be
   substituted), 1½
   pounds each, heads
   off, cleaned
Salt and freshly
   ground pepper to
   taste
4 cloves garlic, 2 thinly
   sliced, 2 minced
20 fresh basil leaves
   (do not substitute
   dried)
15 fresh oregano
   leaves (do not
   substitute dried)
½ cup extra virgin olive
   oil
1 pound ripe cherry
   tomatoes, cut in half
2 cups light fish stock,
   brought to a simmer
10 small new potatoes,
   peeled, blanched in
   boiling salted water
   for 10 minutes

Preheat the oven to 450°F.

Season the insides of the fish with salt and pepper, the sliced garlic, and half the basil and oregano.

In a large, wide, ovenproof pan over medium-high heat, warm the olive oil. Add the tomatoes, then the minced garlic, and season with salt and pepper. Sauté until the tomatoes are wilted, about 4 to 5 minutes, then add the remaining basil and oregano. Add the hot fish stock, and bring the mixture to a boil. Place the fish and the potatoes in the sauce so that they are at least partially covered, cover the pan with a lid or aluminum foil, and transfer to the preheated oven for 10 minutes, or until the fish is just cooked through.

SERVES 2

Fall

Parmesan Gelato

1½ cups heavy cream
1¼ cups grated Parmesan cheese
Pinch of freshly ground pepper
2 ripe pears
½ cup walnut halves
Baguette croutons
1 tablespoon chestnut honey,
   or regular honey

Put the cream, Parmesan cheese, and pepper in a double boiler (a large metal bowl set over a smaller pan of simmering water will do the trick) over low heat and stir continuously with a whisk until the cheese is completely melted, about 15 to 20 minutes. Remove from the heat and pour the mixture through a coarse strainer into a 10-inch oval gratin dish. Let the gelato cool in the refrigerator overnight.

When you're ready to enjoy it, prepare the pears by cutting them in half, scooping out the seeds and the string, and cutting each half lengthwise into thin slices. Arrange each plate with a scoop of the gelato, 2 fanned-out, sliced pear halves, a cluster of walnut halves, and croutons on which you should invite your "guest" to spread the gelato. Top each scoop of gelato with a few drops of honey.

SERVES 2

Semifreddo with Torrone and Orange Sauce

For the semifreddo:

7 ounces torrone (see Note)
1 cup heavy cream
4 eggs, separated
½ cup sugar

For the orange sauce:

1 teaspoon cornstarch
1 tablespoon cold water
4 oranges
⅓ cup sugar
4 tablespoons orange liqueur such as
   Grand Marnier or Cointreau
½ cup dry spumante wine

½ cup thin strips of candied orange
   rind

NOTE: Torrone, which means "nougat," is an Italian candy composed of a hard white shell with an almond in the center. It is available from specialty and gourmet stores.

MAKE THE SEMIFREDDO: Chop the torrone fine. Set aside.

In a mixing bowl, whip the cream until it's thick. In a separate bowl, beat the egg whites until they are very stiff. In another bowl, beat the egg yolks with the sugar until the mixture is creamy. Combine the creamed yolks into the whipped cream. Fold in the egg whites. Fold in the torrone. Pour the batter into four 2½-inch ring-shape molds about 1-inch deep. Place them in the freezer for 2 hours. It is okay to freeze the semifreddo for longer, but if you let it freeze solid, thaw it before serving.

MAKE THE SAUCE: In a cup, mix the cornstarch with the cold water. Squeeze the juice from the oranges into a saucepan. Add the cornstarch mixture, the sugar, liqueur, and wine, and cook over medium heat until the mixture is reduced to a quarter of its original volume, about 2 minutes. It should be thick and syrupy. Remove the sauce from the heat and let it cool to room temperature.

To serve, turn the semifreddo onto dessert plates. Drizzle with the orange sauce, and garnish with the candied orange rind.

SERVES 4; SAVE EXTRA SAUCE FOR ANOTHER USE

A Cooking Party

(Serves 12)

Sometimes I go to dinner at some-one's house, and I think to myself, This person and I should trade places. They should run a restaurant and I should cook for people at home. I think this because a lot of people try to turn their home into a restau-rant by doing everything in the kitchen and treating me like an anony-mous patron, keeping me in the "front of the house" and announcing each phase of the evening. They won't even let me refill my own glass!

I don't follow this practice at home. When my wife and I entertain, we invite our guests to treat our house like their house and make themselves comfortable. Not only is this a more relaxed, friendly way to treat people, but it makes the host's life less stressful as well.

If you have a hard time with this idea, I suggest that you throw a cook-ing party where you invite your guests into the kitchen. Not only will this force you to relax, but it's also a good way to find out how comfortable you are with the recipes you are cook-ing. If it makes you feel naked and insecure to have your friends there watching you, maybe you should try something easier. It's also fun to have a cooking party because everyone can contribute to the meal, which in a season of maturity is a very good approach—making everyone responsible for one part of the evening.

This menu has a lot of fun activi-ties for your guests. The Fried Whitebait in Paper Cones (page 185) and Fried Sage in Beer Batter with Anchovies (page 186) allow them to create two of the few foods in this book that would go with a beer, the perfect drink for such an informal party.

There's always one talented cook in the bunch, and this person should make the desserts—Baby Chocolate and Coffee Truffles (page 190) and Oven-Baked Peach Halves Filled with Chocolate and Amaretti Cookies (page 192)—because those are the most dif-ficult recipes to manage.

There's only one problem when everyone cooks: There's nobody left to clean up. But hopefully your guests will feel a mature sense of obligation here as well.

Fried Whitebait in Paper Cones

2 pounds whitebait
2 cups flour, for dusting
1 quart vegetable oil, for frying
Salt to taste

Rinse and pat the fish dry. Dust the fish with the flour, then shake off the excess using a strainer. In a deep pan over medium-high heat, warm the oil until it reaches 375°F. (a drop of water will crackle and sputter). Fry the fish until it's gold and crispy in small batches, so as not to crowd the pan and to keep the oil at the proper temperature. As each batch is ready, after about 1 minute, lift it from the pan with a slotted spoon or skimmer onto a plate lined with paper towels. Season to taste with salt and let the oil drain onto the paper.

Shape sheets of butcher paper into cones and serve the fried whitebait in the cones.

SERVES 12

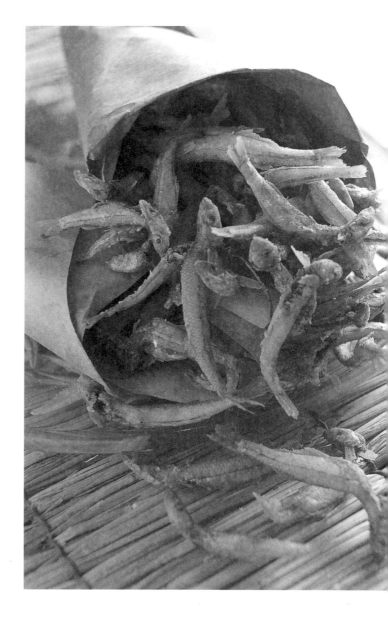

Fried Sage in Beer Batter with Anchovies

5 anchovy fillets

50 fresh sage leaves

2 cups all-purpose flour

½ cup beer

1 cup seltzer water

2 eggs, separated

Pinch of salt

Vegetable oil, for frying

Cut each anchovy into 5 pieces. Sandwich each piece of anchovy between 2 sage leaves. Press together to seal.

In a mixing bowl, whisk together the flour, beer, seltzer, and egg yolks. The mixture should be the consistency of heavy cream. In a separate bowl, whisk the egg whites with a pinch of salt until they form stiff peaks. Fold the egg whites into the beer batter with a rubber spatula.

Fill a deep, heavy pan with 3 inches of oil. Warm it over medium-high heat until it reach 375°F. (a drop of water will sizzle and splatter). Holding the leaves by the stem, dip each one into the batter. Deep-fry the sandwiches to a light golden color, about 3 minutes. Remove with a slotted spoon and drain on paper towels.

Simply Tuscan

Serves 12

Crostini with
Fagioli al Fiasco

For the topping:

2 cups dried cannellini beans
   (white kidneys)
3 cloves garlic, crushed
6 fresh sage leaves
6 tablespoons extra virgin
   olive oil
Pinch of salt

For the crostini:

1 baguette, sliced
1 clove garlic, cut in half
1 bunch fresh basil, washed
   and dried
Freshly ground black pepper
   to taste

water from time to time to keep the beans submerged, but you should end up with beans in a thick sauce.

MAKE THE TOPPING: In a bowl, cover the cannellini with water and soak them overnight or all day. Drain the beans. Cover them by 1 inch with fresh water in a large, heavy pan. Add the crushed garlic, sage, olive oil, and salt. Bring to a boil, then reduce the heat and simmer slowly until the beans are soft and the water is almost entirely absorbed, about 15 minutes. You may have to add boiling

MAKE THE CROSTINI: When the beans are ready and you are ready to serve, toast the bread until pale brown in a 200°F. oven. While the bread is still warm, rub each slice with the open end of the garlic halves. Slather each slice with cooked beans. Garnish each slice with a basil leaf and freshly ground pepper.

SERVES 12

Fall

Fava Bean Soup with Farro and Dandelion

½ cup extra virgin olive oil

1 cup chopped onion

1 pound dried, peeled split favas

Salt and freshly ground pepper to
    taste

1 cup dry farro (see page 111),
    soaked overnight, blanched 15
    minutes until slightly soft, and
    drained

2 pounds dandelion greens, stalky
    leaves removed and discarded,
    washed thoroughly, and coarsely
    chopped

1 clove garlic, minced

In a heavy pot or casserole over medium-high heat, warm 2 tablespoons of the olive oil. Add the onion and cook until translucent, about 5 minutes. Add the fava beans and cover with water. Add salt and pepper and bring to a boil. Reduce the heat to low, add the farro, and simmer, uncovered, for 20 minutes. Add the dandelion greens and cook for another 20 minutes, until the favas are beginning to fall apart. Remove from the heat, stir in the garlic, and serve, garnishing each serving with some of the remaining olive oil and freshly ground black pepper.

SERVES   6

Strozzapreti

Ricotta and Spinach Dumplings
with Pancetta, Arugula, and Balsamic Vinegar

For the dumplings

1 pound fresh spinach leaves, washed
  carefully

1 pound ricotta impastata (a dry fresh
  ricotta—if unavailable, buy regular
  fresh ricotta and drain the excess
  water by hanging the cheese over
  the sink in cheesecloth, or in a
  cheesecloth-lined colander, for
  30 minutes)

2½ cups all-purpose flour

1 egg

¼ cup grated Parmesan cheese

½ teaspoon grated nutmeg

Salt and freshly ground pepper
  to taste

For the sauce:

2 tablespoons olive oil

4 ounces pancetta, cut into ½-inch
  cubes

4 shallots, peeled and chopped

2 bunches of arugula, washed carefully
  and cut into ¼-inch julienne

1 tablespoon unsalted butter, cut into
  fingertip-size pieces

4 tablespoons freshly grated Parmesan
  cheese

2 tablespoons balsamic vinegar
  (see Note)

NOTE: Use only authentic Aceto Balsamico Tradizionale di Modena.

MAKE THE DUMPLINGS: Bring a pot of salted water to a boil. Blanch the spinach for 1 minute. Drain the spinach, let it cool off enough to handle, then squeeze out all the excess water. Chop the spinach and mix it with the ricotta, ⅞ cup of the flour, and the egg, Parmesan, nutmeg, and salt and pepper. It should form a firm, smooth, non-sticky dough. Reserve the remaining ¾ cup of flour for dusting the table or thickening the dough.

Dust a section of your work surface with flour and roll a small piece (a generous tablespoon) of the dough into a log ¾ inch in diameter. Cut the log into 1½-inch lengths and roll each piece between your palms to taper the ends. Repeat with the remaining dough.

continued

Bring a pot of salted water to a boil. Drop in the dumplings. They are ready when they float to the top, about 2 to 3 minutes. Drain at this point. While the strozzapreti are boiling, prepare the sauce.

MAKE THE SAUCE: In a large, wide pan over high heat, warm the olive oil. Add the pancetta and shallots and sauté until the pancetta is crispy, about 4 minutes. Add the arugula and the drained strozzapreti and toss well. Add the butter, Parmesan, and balsamic vinegar, toss again, and serve immediately.

SERVES 12

Baby Chocolate and Coffee Truffles

11 ounces bittersweet chocolate
1/2 cup heavy cream
1/4 cup unsweetened cocoa powder
1 short espresso (brewed strong, with less water than usual)
7/8 cup sweetened cocoa powder

Cut the chocolate into small chunks. Melt the chunks in a double boiler (a bowl set over a pan of simmering water). When the chocolate has melted, about 10 to 12 minutes, remove the bowl from the pan. Add a little cream to the unsweetened cocoa and mix with a spoon to make a paste, then thin the paste by adding the rest of the cream, mixing continually with a whisk. Add the cocoa cream to the melted chocolate and blend thoroughly. Let the mixture cool in the refrigerator until cold, about 1 hour.

Beat the espresso into the mixture with an electric mixer or an egg beater, keeping the bowl cold by setting it in an ice water bath. When it is well blended, smooth, and creamy, dust your hands with the sweet cocoa powder and use them to form the mixture into small (1/2-inch) balls, keeping your hands dusted the whole time and placing the balls in little paper confectioner's cups.

MAKES 24 LITTLE TRUFFLES

Oven-Baked Peach Halves Filled
with Chocolate and Amaretti Cookies

4 fresh, ripe peaches, halved
   and pitted
1 egg
1 tablespoon unsweetened
   cocoa powder
1 tablespoon sugar
8 amaretti cookies, crumbled

Preheat the oven to 300°F.

Scrape a tablespoon or so of pulp from the inside of each peach half. Chop the pulp. In a medium bowl, beat the egg. Add the chopped peach pulp, and all the other ingredients except the peach halves. Mix well. Place the peach halves, open side up, on a baking sheet. Spoon the peach pulp mixture into and over the peach halves. Bake the peaches in the preheated oven for 30 minutes, or until the peaches are cooked through but still firm, and golden brown on top.

SERVES 8

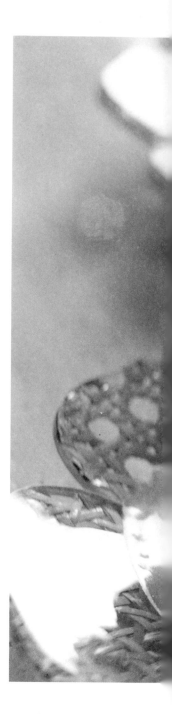

A Business Dinner
(Serves 6)

Perhaps fall is the perfect season to invite some people you work with to your home, treat them to a meal, and get to know them a little better. I haven't worked in many offices except my own, but it seems to me that people just aren't themselves at work, especially in the United States. Everyone is so concerned with their image that it's difficult to really get to know them.

Then there are those people who really are what they seem to be at work—unhappy souls trapped in their suits, who simply do nothing but make phone calls, write memos, and go to meetings—as if that were all there is. They eat bad meals on the run, good meals only when it's to do business, and they never enjoy themselves. The phrase "get a life" comes to mind.

Well, this is a meal that could get even those people to stop and smell the roses for a few minutes because they'll be so pleasantly surprised by the food you present to them. The key is to disorient them with pleasure, and remind them of the senses they've smothered by locking them away inside their suits and choking them with their neckties.

This meal begins with a Veal Shank Salad (page 196) whose green sauce and pickled onion will wake up the palates of your guests. I'm sure they've never had such a salad, and they'll be lost in pleasure as they discover it bite by bite.

Next comes a Cherry Tomato and Pecorino Farrotto (page 198) that has a very rustic flavor and aroma—a total change of pace that will take them in another direction entirely. If they haven't been drinking wine yet, they'll start with this dish. Pour them a big, bold red and make them take off that tie!

For a main course, the Warm Capon Breast with Spinach Mashed Potatoes (page 199) will definitely hold their interest. This is a hearty, succulent, satisfying dish that demands attention. Your guests will eat it slowly, drink some more wine, and—I promise you—end the meal smiling like you've never seen them do before.

Finally, the Rice Ice Cream with Mixed Berries Sauce (page 203) boasts bright colors and a creamy texture. It has a childlike quality that just might make everyone feel a little less formal. Perhaps a co-worker will loosen up and invite you over for a meal sometime soon, or stop and watch the sun set the next day. Probably not, but you never know. . . .

Veal Shank Salad

1 whole veal shank

1 yellow onion, peeled

1 carrot, peeled

1 stalk celery, washed

1 bouquet garni (2 bay leaves, 6 whole
cloves, 1 tablespoon black
peppercorns, wrapped and tied
in cheesecloth)

½ cup kosher salt

1½ pounds Yukon Gold potatoes,
peeled and cut into ½-inch dice

One 10½-ounce jar cornichons,
drained and cut into ¼-inch slices

One 10½-ounce jar pickled onions,
drained

½ teaspoon salt

⅞ cup red wine vinegar

1⅓ cups extra virgin olive oil

5 ounces cleaned and rinsed frisee

5 ounces cleaned and dried fresh
parsley leaves

1 tablespoon drained capers

1 shallot, peeled

2 hard-boiled eggs, peeled

Put the veal shank in a pot with the onion, carrot, celery, and bouquet garni. Cover with cold water and add the kosher salt. Bring to a boil over high heat, then reduce the heat to medium-low and simmer for 45 minutes, or until the meat is tender. Let the shank cool in the cooking liquid.

Meanwhile, bring a pot of lightly salted water to a boil and cook the potatoes until fork tender, about 10 minutes. Remove them from the water with a slotted spoon and cool them in ice water for a few minutes, then take them out and let them dry on a clean kitchen towel.

When the shank has cooled to room temperature, remove all the meat from the bone, using a sharp paring knife. Cut the meat into ¾-inch dice. Mix the meat in a bowl with the potatoes, all but 2 tablespoons of the cornichons, and all but 2 tablespoons of the pickled onions. Set aside the reserved cornichons and pickled onions. In a bowl, use a whisk to dissolve the salt in 3 tablespoons of the red wine vinegar. Whisk in ⅓ cup of the extra virgin olive oil until it is emulsified. Pour half the dressing over the

meat salad and mix thoroughly.
Pour the remainder over the
frisee and toss well.

Put the parsley, the reserved
cornichons and pickled onions,
the capers, shallot, hard-boiled
eggs, and the remainder of the
red wine vinegar and olive oil
into the bowl of a processor.
Pulse to obtain a coarse but
well-blended sauce.

Serve by plating the frisee,
mounding the meat salad over it,
and topping with green sauce.

Serves 6

Cherry Tomato and Pecorino

Farrotto

⅓ cup extra virgin olive oil

2 cloves garlic, finely chopped

1 pound ripe cherry tomatoes, halved

10 basil leaves

Pinch of crushed hot red pepper

Salt and freshly ground pepper
   to taste

3 cups farro (see page 111), blanched
   15 minutes until it just begins to
   soften, drained, and drizzled with
   olive oil

5 cups vegetable broth or stock, kept
   on the simmer

8 tablespoons freshly grated pecorino
   Toscano cheese (substitute with
   young manchego if necessary), plus
   12 thinly shaved slices

In a wide, heavy saucepan over medium-high heat, warm 2 tablespoons of the olive oil. Add the garlic and sauté until it turns brown, about 3 minutes. Add the tomatoes, half the basil, the hot red pepper, and salt and pepper. Add the drained farro, reduce the heat to medium, mix well to coat the grains, and add a ladle of the broth. Cook the farro, stirring often to prevent sticking, and adding a ladle of broth every time the liquid is absorbed. Cook until al dente, about 20 minutes total. Add the grated pecorino, and the remaining basil and olive oil, stirring vigorously until the <u>farrotto</u> is creamy. Top each serving with pecorino shavings.

SERVES 4 TO 6

Warm Capon Breast with Spinach Mashed Potatoes

For the capon:

1 capon breast
Salt and freshly ground pepper
  to taste
6 tablespoons unsalted butter
2 sprigs fresh rosemary

For the sauce:

½ teaspoon salt
4 tablespoons very good aged balsamic
  vinegar (see Note)
⅓ cup extra virgin olive oil
Grated zest of 2 lemons
½ cup golden raisins, soaked in warm
  water for 30 minutes to plump, then
  drained
½ cup pine nuts

**For the spinach mashed
potatoes:**

1 pound spinach, cleaned, rinsed, and
  spun dry
1 pound Idaho potatoes
¾ pound unsalted butter
½ cup hot whole milk
½ cup freshly grated Parmigiano-
  Reggiano

1 teaspoon grated nutmeg
Salt to taste

*NOTE: Use only authentic Aceto Bal-
samico Tradizionale di Modena.*

PREPARE THE CAPON: Preheat the
oven to 400°F. Rub the capon breast
all over with salt and pepper. Use
some of the butter to grease a baking
pan lightly, and dot the capon breast
with the remaining butter. Lay the
rosemary sprigs on top, cover it
tightly with foil, and cook it in the
preheated oven for 20 minutes. Remove
the foil and continue cooking for
another 15 minutes, until the capon
breast turns golden brown. The capon
is finished when it feels springy to
the touch. Remove from the oven and
set it aside.

PREPARE THE SAUCE: Dissolve the
salt in the balsamic vinegar by whisking them together in a bowl. Add the
olive oil, lemon zest, drained
raisins, pine nuts, and 4 tablespoons
of the liquid from the bottom of the
roasting pan, and whisk them all
together.

continued

Fall

199

PREPARE THE SPINACH
MASHED POTATOES: In a pot,
steam the spinach leaves for 4
minutes, squeeze them dry, and
chop them fine with a knife.
Boil the potatoes in a pot of
lightly salted water, then
drain and peel them. Pass them
through a food mill or potato
ricer, then put them back in
the pot over very low heat.
Add the butter, milk, and
Parmigiano-Reggiano. Whisk vigorously with a wooden spoon.
Stir in the spinach and mix
until evenly amalgamated; add
the nutmeg and adjust the seasoning with salt.

To serve, arrange the spinach
mashed potatoes in a mound in
the center of each plate.
Slice the capon breast into $1/4$-
inch-thick slices and place the
slices on top of the potatoes.
Spoon the sauce over and
around the capon and the
mashed potatoes.

SERVES 6

Pears Poached in Vernaccia Wine, Stuffed with Gorgonzola and Mascarpone

6 medium-ripe pears

2 cups Vernaccia (or other dry white) wine

1 cinnamon stick

6 ounces Gorgonzola cheese, at room temperature

3 ounces mascarpone cheese, at room temperature

Peel and core the pears, leaving them whole; place them in a casserole large and deep enough to fit them in a single layer. Pour in the wine and add the cinnamon stick. Cook the pears, covered, over medium heat until cooked through but still firm, about 8 to 10 minutes, cool them to room temperature.

Place the 2 cheeses in a bowl and mix them with a whisk until well blended and fluffy. Fill the pears with the cheese mixture and serve at room temperature.

S E R V E S 6

Rice Ice Cream with Mixed Berries Sauce

For the ice cream:

3½ cups milk

⅔ cup Carnaroli rice (you may
  substitute arborio rice)

4 egg yolks

6 tablespoons sugar

1 egg white, whipped to stiff peaks

2 cups heavy cream, whipped until stiff

For the sauce:

4 tablespoons unsalted butter

2 tablespoons dark brown sugar

2 cups mixed berries (select whatever
  is seasonal)

¼ cup Grand Marnier liqueur

1 cup red wine

2 tablespoons granulated sugar

¼ cup kirsch

MAKE THE ICE CREAM: In a saucepan over medium heat, warm the milk. When it's hot, but not boiling, stir in the rice. Simmer, uncovered, until the rice is soft, about 30 minutes. Remove the pan from the heat and let the rice cool to room temperature. Off the heat, cream the egg yolks and sugar in a separate, larger saucepan. Fold the beaten egg white into the egg yolk and sugar mixture, then add the cooked rice and milk. Put the pan on very low heat and cook, stirring constantly, until the mixture starts to thicken. Do not let the contents reach the boiling point. When it begins to thicken, remove the pan from the heat and let it cool down, stirring frequently. When it reaches room temperature again, fold in the whipped cream, then transfer the contents to an ice cream machine and follow the manufacturer's instructions. If you do not have an ice cream machine, put the mixture in the freezer for an hour, stirring every 15 minutes.

MAKE THE SAUCE: In a skillet over medium heat, melt the butter. Stir in the brown sugar. When the brown sugar dissolves, add the berries and stir to coat them. Add the Grand Marnier and let it reduce for 5 minutes. Add the red wine, granulated sugar, and kirsch, reduce the heat to low, and cook until the liquid is reduced and the sauce is moist and creamy, about 20 minutes.

Serve the ice cream with the warm sauce ladled on top.

SERVES 6

Fall

San Gimignano
Pitigliano
Montepulciano

Tuscany

Pisa

Firenze

Lucca

Siena

Winter

Snowy Endings and New Beginnings

It had begun to snow again. He watched sleepily the flakes, silver and dark, falling obliquely against the lamplight. . . . It lay thickly drifted on the crooked crosses and headstones, on the spears of the little gate, on the barren thorns. His soul swooned slowly as he heard the snow falling faintly through the universe and faintly falling, like the descent of their last end, upon all the living and the dead.

—JAMES JOYCE,
The Dead

When winter settles in and the first big snowfall comes, I find myself in a small Italian town called Bolzano. At least I do in my mind. The year is 1975 and I am happy because I'm a young actor and, as an early Christmas present, the Fates have placed me under contract to a theater company in this charming little mountain community. In fact, I'm in such a good mood that I don't even mind there's a snowstorm outside—a furious onslaught of whitened wind that commands all of us to stay indoors. I don't even mind being alone in my room. I'm content to give in to the cold, and I pour myself a glass of wine and turn on the television. The headline story freezes this moment in my mind forever: The anchorman announces that Pier Paolo Pasolini is dead, murdered that afternoon by a group of young male prostitutes.

You've probably never heard of Pasolini, but, to my generation of Italians, and to quite a few American baby boomers, he was a folk hero—an intellectual revolutionary who used his poems, films, and other creations to behave like a sane Don Quixote, passionately tilting at windmills that he knew would never topple. There are no comparable artistic figures in America. Instead you have to look for political comparisons, and I would say that Pier Paolo was, to me and my friends, what Martin Luther King, Jr., and Malcolm X were to African Americans. And, like those two gentlemen, he was killed before his time by people who feared him.

I think of Pier Paolo every winter and I think of him especially when it snows. And I think how perfect the phrase "dead of winter" is for summing up what this season is all about.

I can hear you now. "Stop!" you are saying. "This is a sad story. What is it doing here with all of these recipes? Aren't the holidays a time for celebration?"

Of course they are. But let's be honest—the winter is a sad time. Winter is somber. Winter is a time for solitude and reflection and winter is—let's be <u>really</u> honest— the time of death. But here again, I remember the Tuscan idea of the endless cycle of life, and I know that there is a light at the end of the tunnel.

That light is the New Year, which is a time for renewal, a chance to start over and live another year. I often think of the new year in terms of walking down a snowy path. Will I simply retrace my footsteps in the snow, I wonder, or will I have the courage to go in a different direction, maybe taking a better route. I usually end up trying a new path, thinking to myself, "This time I'm going to get it right."

A Quintessential
Winter Menu

A Quintessential Winter Menu
(Serves 4)

In the winter, we need food more than at any other time of year. During this season, it keeps us warm and nourishes us against the cold. Food is like the embrace of a loved one; it revives our senses if they've been dulled by the "dead of winter."

There are several mandatory dishes during the Tuscan winter, but many of them require you to be a Tuscan in order to enjoy them. For example, a

Castagnaccio, a chestnut flour tart with flavors of rosemary, pine nuts, and olive oil, is special to Tuscans, but if you're not a Tuscan it may seem too dry. So, in the spirit of the holidays, I've replaced it here with a recipe for Apple Roll (page 218) that was handed down by Marta's grandmother. Trust me: As much as you might think you want to try an authentic Tuscan dessert, this one, in the Tuscan spirit, will please you much more on a cold winter's day. Having said that, I _have_ included some very traditional Tuscan fare. For example, the Sweet and Sour Wild Boar with Chestnut Gnocchi (page 216) represents the Tuscan winter with dark intense flavors and herbs. It's exactly the kind of thing you'd want to be served after coming in from a hike in the woods of Montalcino.

Similarly, the Braised Quail and Caramelized Shallots with Soft Polenta (page 212) is a hearty dinner that will warm you on even the coldest winter day. And the Garganelli with Truffle-Scented Fondue (page 214) will ignite your senses on days when extra stimulation is required.

Braised Quail and Caramelized Shallots
with Soft Polenta

For the polenta:

4½ cups water
Salt to taste
1 cup polenta
1 tablespoon extra virgin olive oil

For the quail:

4 cleaned quail, breastbones removed
Salt and freshly ground pepper to
  taste

4 bay leaves
4 slices pancetta
4 tablespoons extra virgin olive oil
½ cup dry white wine
½ cup chicken stock
16 whole shallots, peeled and blanched
  in boiling water for 30 seconds

MAKE THE POLENTA: You can either
follow the instructions on the package
or use these instructions: In a deep,
heavy pan, bring the water, lightly

salted, to a boil. Reduce the heat to medium. Beating continually with a whisk, add the polenta slowly and gradually. Stir constantly as you cook the polenta until it reaches the consistency of a creamy porridge, about 5 minutes. Stir in salt to taste and a tablespoon of extra virgin olive oil, then cover and set the polenta aside in a warm place until you are ready to serve.

MAKE THE QUAIL: Preheat the oven to 400°F. Season the quail inside and out with salt and pepper, and place a bay leaf inside each one. Wrap each quail in a slice of pancetta, securing it with a toothpick. In a wide, ovenproof skillet over medium-high heat, warm the olive oil. Cook the quail until they are lightly browned with crisp skin, 3 to 4 minutes on each side. Sprinkle the wine over the quail. When the wine has evaporated, add the chicken stock and the shallots. Cover the pan with foil or an ovenproof lid and place it in the preheated oven. After 5 minutes, uncover, then cook for another 5 minutes. Remove the pan from the oven. Remove the quail and set them aside in a warm place. Skim the fat from the pan, then let the remaining juices simmer over low heat until they are reduced by half and the shallots are brown and burnished, 15 to 20 minutes, stirring

up the brown bits from the bottom of the pan.

To serve, divide the polenta among 4 wide soup bowls. Place a quail on top of each bed of polenta and spoon the shallots and sauce over the birds.

SERVES 4

Garganelli with Truffle-Scented Fondue

3½ ounces fontina Val D'Aosta
    cheese, cut into ¼-inch dice
2 tablespoons flour
1½ cups milk, or more as needed
4 egg yolks
2 tablespoons unsalted butter, cut into
    small pieces and kept cold
1 large Spanish onion, baked in its skin
    in a 300° F. oven for 1 hour, then
    peeled and cut into ½-inch cubes
Salt and freshly ground pepper
    to taste
2 pinches of grated nutmeg
1 tablespoon chopped fresh rosemary
1 pound garganelli (use fusilli if
    unavailable)
1 white truffle (about 1½ ounces)

In a mixing bowl, sprinkle the flour over the fontina. Add the milk. If the cheese isn't covered, add more milk to cover. Let the mixture soak for a minimum of 4 hours, or for up to 24 hours, in the refrigerator.

Make a double boiler by setting the bowl of cheese and milk over a saucepan half full of water placed over medium-low heat. Whisk constantly until the cheese is melted. Then add the egg yolks, one at a time, still whisking. Finally, add the cold diced butter gradually, still whisking. Continue to whisk until the mixture reaches the consistency of pastry cream, 5 to 10 minutes. Remove the pan from the heat, but keep the bowl on it.

Bring a large pot of salted water to a boil for the pasta. While the water is coming to a boil, put the diced, baked onion in a large, wide pan over low heat. Season it with salt and pepper, the nutmeg, rosemary, and 2 tablespoons of the boiling water. After 5 minutes, turn off the heat and pour the fondue in gradually, beating with a whisk to incorporate it. Warm the fondue until it is hot to the touch but not boiling. Do not let it come to a boil, or it will curdle.

Add the garganelli to the boiling water and cook until al dente. Drain the pasta and add it to the fondue. Remove the pan from the heat and mix it well. Divide among 4 plates, and shave some of the truffle on top of each serving.

SERVES 4

Simply Tuscan

214

Sweet and Sour Wild Boar with Chestnut Gnocchi

For the boar:

2 pounds boar meat, from the leg or
   shoulder, cut into 1-inch cubes
   (see Note)
1 bottle full-bodied red wine
1 bouquet garni (2 bay leaves, a sprig
   of fresh thyme, 2 whole cloves, a
   3-inch cinnamon stick, 3 cloves
   garlic, 1 tablespoon juniper berries,
   and 1 teaspoon black peppercorns,
   all wrapped together in cheesecloth)
½ cup olive oil
½ cup chopped onion
½ cup chopped carrot
½ cup chopped celery
Salt and freshly ground pepper
   to taste
½ cup dried sour cherries
½ cup beef or vegetable broth, as
   needed
¼ cup unsweetened cocoa powder
4 tablespoons water

For the sweet and sour sauce:

⅔ cup sugar
2 cloves garlic, crushed
2 bay leaves

3 tablespoons water
3 tablespoons red wine vinegar

Chestnut Gnocchi (recipe follows)

NOTE: Wild boar is available at
gourmet shops; you may use buffalo or
lamb as a substitute.

MAKE THE BOAR: Marinate the meat
overnight in the red wine with the
bouquet garni. The next day, lift the
meat out of the marinade with a slotted spoon and pat it dry with paper
towels. Reserve the marinade. In a
large casserole over medium-low heat,
warm half the olive oil. Add the
chopped vegetables and let them sweat
until the onions are translucent,
about 5 minutes. Meanwhile, warm the
remaining olive oil in a skillet over
high heat. Add the meat and sear it on
all sides. Add the seared meat to the
vegetables and season with salt and
pepper. Add the reserved marinade,
including the bouquet garni, and the
sour cherries to the casserole, turn
the heat to high, and bring to a boil.
When it reaches a boil, reduce the
heat to low, cover partially, and simmer until the meat is tender, about 90
minutes. At this point, dissolve the

cocoa in the water and add it to the casserole. There should be a lot of juice from the meat. If it's not juicy, add some broth to keep it moist.

MAKE THE SWEET AND SOUR SAUCE: In a skillet over low heat, simmer the sugar, garlic, and bay leaves, along with the water, until the sugar lique- fies, about 3 minutes. When the sugar is golden, add the red wine vinegar. The sugar will harden and stick to the bottom of the pan. Keep on simmering over very low heat until the sugar melts again. Stir this mixture into the casserole and let it simmer for 15 minutes more. Serve with the chestnut gnocchi.

SERVES 4

Chestnut Gnocchi

2 pounds Idaho potatoes

1½ cups "00" flour (see Note), or use all-purpose flour as a substitute

5 ounces chestnut flour

2 eggs

½ cup freshly grated Parmesan cheese

1 teaspoon grated nutmeg

Salt and freshly ground pepper to taste

8 tablespoons unsalted butter

8 leaves fresh sage

NOTE: This high-gluten flour proofs extremely well. Purchase it in spe- cialty stores or Italian markets.

In a pot of salted water, boil the potatoes until they are fork tender, about 10 to 12 minutes, then peel them and pass them through a ricer. On a clean work surface, mound the mashed potatoes and make a well in the cen- ter. Place all the remaining ingredients, except the butter and sage, in the well. Mix it together until it forms a homogenous dough. Knead the dough until it is smooth. If it is sticky, add a little more flour.

Divide the dough into 4 portions and roll each portion into a ½-inch-wide

continued

Winter

log. Cut the log into 1-inch pieces.
(A dough scraper is a good tool to use
for this.) Place the gnocchi on a
floured tray as you cut them. Cook the
gnocchi in a large pot of boiling
salted water until they float, 3 to 4
minutes, then lift them out gently
with a slotted spoon.

While the gnocchi are cooking, melt
the butter in a sauté pan over low
heat. Add the sage. Toss the cooked
and drained gnocchi with the sage butter.

S E R V E S   4

Marta's Grandmother's Apple Roll

2¼ cups flour

1 egg

12 tablespoons butter, softened to room
   temperature

¼ cup hot milk

Pinch of salt

2 pounds tart apples, such as Italian
   Renette or Granny Smith

⅝ cup sugar

½ cup raisins, soaked in warm water
   for 30 minutes or until plump

¾ cup pine nuts

¾ cup walnut halves

Grated zest of 1 lemon

Place the flour on a clean work surface. Make a well in the center. Put
the egg, 2 tablespoons of butter, half
the milk, and the salt in the well.
Using a fork, pull some of the flour
into the center and mix it with the
egg. Continue pulling a little flour
into the center and mixing it together
until it is all incorporated into a
smooth dough. Add more milk, a spoonful at a time, if there is not enough
liquid to absorb the flour. Wrap the
dough in plastic and let it rest while
you are preparing the apples.

Peel, core, and cut the apples into 8 wedges each. Sprinkle them with 2 tablespoons of the sugar and let them rest. Roll out the dough with a rolling pin on a clean surface dusted with flour, into a circular shape about 1/8 inch thick. Spread the apples out evenly on the dough. Squeeze the raisins to release excess water and strew them over the apples, along with the pine nuts, walnuts, and lemon zest. Sprinkle all but 1/4 cup of the remaining sugar over the top. Then melt 6 tablespoons of butter and drizzle it evenly over all.

Preheat the oven to 300°F. Grease a cookie sheet with butter.

Beginning at one end, roll this mixture loosely into a thick log. Bring the ends together to form a ring. Using both hands, spread out to act like spatulas, gently lift the roll onto the sheet, then dot it with the remaining 4 tablespoons of butter and sprinkle the remaining 1/4 cup of sugar over it. Put the roll in the preheated oven. When the roll forms a dry crust on the outside (after about 30 minutes), if the apples have not released juice into the bottom of the pan, add enough water to cover the bottom of the pan by 1/8 inch. Using a spoon, baste the roll every 10 minutes with the liquid in the bottom of the pan to caramelize the surface. The roll is cooked when the surface is crisp and golden brown, about another 30 minutes. As soon as the roll is done, remove it from the pan immediately; otherwise, it will stick to the bottom. To remove the roll, cover it with a lid and invert it so that it is sitting upside down on the lid; then perform the same inversion trick to get it right side up on a serving platter.

SERVES 6

Christmas Eve and Christmas Day
(Serves 6)

There may not be a more drastic indicator of the differences between Tuscany and the United States than the way the two cultures celebrate Christmas. Think about it: The holiday has the same origin, but it is handled so differently in these two places that it's like twins separated at birth and raised in two different places—one (the Tuscan) in the country and the other (the American) on Madison Avenue.

During the holidays, my house is like a laboratory where some scientist has decided to see which is more powerful, the Tuscan gene (mine) or the American (my wife's); the masculine strength of the patriarch, or the combined will of a woman and three children.

Does it surprise you to learn that we have an American Christmas in our home?

So this is something else I mourn in the winter—my own past, the way things used to be for me. In Tuscany, there's a ritual called the Lettera a Babbo Natale, which is a letter that the children write to their father telling him how good they've been for the year, which will determine what kind of present they'll receive on Twelfth Night. The letter is read at Christmas lunch and it's usually a big production, with the father acting surprised to find it under his plate. On Christmas Day, I think of all the Italian fathers playing out this part and—though I am happy to be with my family—I feel sad to be so far away from my other home.

It's because of my longings for Italy at this time of year that I make several of the dishes featured here. For example, the Orange and Fennel Salad (page 222) is more Sicilian than Tuscan, but it's so Tuscan in spirit that it's exactly the kind of thing I would eat for refreshment during a Tuscan winter. The Farfalline with Walnuts, Cinnamon, and Lemon Zest (page 224), on the other hand, is vintage Tuscan—a flood season dish really, because you would be likely to find all of the necessary ingredients in a Tuscan pantry on any day of the year.

But, to be honest, I cannot deny the pleasure I take in the American Christmas. Watching the joy in my children's eyes as they walk through Rockefeller Center looking at the Christmas tree and the skating rink, or as they open their presents, how can I resist giving in? It's as much a way of relieving the "dead of winter" as I can think of . . . even if only for a few hours.

Christmas Eve Dinner

Orange and Fennel Salad

2 pounds bulb fennel
1 pound oranges
½ teaspoon salt
Juice of 1 lemon
Juice of 1 orange
¼ cup extra virgin olive oil

30 oil-cured black olives, pitted
1 teaspoon dried oregano

Trim the stem ends and any bruised outer leaves from the fennel. Slice the fennel very thin, crosswise (a mandoline or other slicer will work best—if you use a knife, just slice as thin as you can). Place the fennel slices in a bowl of ice water.

Peel the oranges and divide them into sections. Using a sharp paring knife, remove the membrane surrounding each segment.

In a bowl, whisk the salt into the lemon and orange juice until the salt has dissolved. Add the olive oil and whisk until emulsified.

Drain the fennel slices and shake them dry. Place them in a large bowl with the orange segments, the black olives, and the oregano, and pour the vinaigrette over all. Mix thoroughly but gently and serve either on a platter or individually plated.

SERVES 6

Anchovy Tart

¾ pound ripe cherry tomatoes

1½ teaspoons salt

½ teaspoon sugar

2 tablespoons chopped fresh rosemary

1 tablespoon chopped fresh thyme

2 cloves garlic, sliced thin

1 pound Idaho potatoes

1 pound fresh anchovies or small fresh
    sardines

¼ cup extra virgin olive oil, plus a little
    for greasing the pan

⅓ cup freshly grated pecorino Romano
    cheese

1 teaspoon dried oregano

3 tablespoons bread crumbs

Preheat a convection oven to 200°F., or a regular oven to 300°F. Cut the cherry tomatoes in half and place them cut side up on a sheet pan. Mix the salt with the sugar and sprinkle the mixture evenly over the cherry tomatoes. Top with the rosemary, thyme, and garlic. Dry the tomatoes in the preheated convection oven for 45 minutes, or in the preheated regular oven for an hour, with the door propped open an inch with a cork. In either case, the tomatoes should lose most of their moisture, but should still be slightly moist and meaty.

Peel the potatoes and boil them in a pot of lightly salted water until they're fork tender, about 10 to 12 minutes. Strain them, and when they are cool, cut them into ½-inch-thick slices. Open up the anchovies. Remove and discard from each the head and the central bone, leaving the 2 fillets attached at the back.

Preheat the (regular) oven to 350°F. Grease a 12-inch round ovenproof dish (or the equivalent—something you feel good about bringing to the table) lightly with olive oil.

Scallop the potatoes on the bottom of the dish. Top with the oven-dried tomatoes. Sprinkle with half the pecorino and half the oregano. Drizzle with 2 tablespoons of the olive oil. Top with the anchovies in a single layer. Mix the remaining pecorino with the bread crumbs and sprinkle the mixture over the anchovies. Finish with the remaining oregano, and finally the remaining olive oil. Bake in the preheated oven until the tart is golden brown and crisp on top, 20 to 25 minutes.

SERVES 6

Winter

Farfalline with Walnuts, Cinnamon, and Lemon Zest

1¼ pounds dry farfalline (bow-tie
  pasta)
1 cup coarsely chopped walnuts
1 tablespoon sugar
Grated zest of 1 lemon
¼ teaspoon ground cinnamon
¼ teaspoon grated nutmeg
1½ tablespoons butter
6 tablespoons freshly grated Parmesan
  cheese

Bring a pot of salted water to a
boil. Cook the pasta until it is al
dente.

While the pasta is cooking, mix the
walnuts with the sugar, half the lemon
zest and half the spices. When the
pasta is ready, drain it, toss it with
the butter in a large bowl, then add
the walnut mixture. Toss to mix all
the ingredients thoroughly. Arrange
the pasta on a platter, and sprinkle
the remaining lemon zest and spices
over it. Top each serving with 1
tablespoon of the grated Parmesan.

SERVES 6

Red Snapper in Salt Crust and <u>Salmoriglio</u>

For the fish:

6 pounds kosher salt
1 whole snapper, about 4 pounds,
    insides cleaned but scales left on
1 sprig fresh rosemary
½ lemon, cut into ¼-inch slices

For the <u>salmoriglio</u>:

1 cup extra virgin olive oil
⅓ cup warm water
Juice of 2 lemons
1 clove garlic, crushed
1 tablespoon chopped fresh oregano
1 small bunch of Italian parsley,
    stemmed and chopped
Salt and freshly ground pepper to
    taste

MAKE THE FISH: Preheat the oven to
450°F. Spread a large sheet of foil
inside a roasting pan. Make a bed for
the fish in the foil using half the
salt. Fill the fish cavity with the
rosemary sprig and lemon slices. Place
the fish on the salt bed and lift up
the edges of the foil to contain the
salt in a shape that suggests that of
the fish. Cover the fish with the
remaining salt, and sprinkle water
over it so that the salt sticks
together (this should require about ¼
cup of water). Bake in the preheated
oven for 30 minutes. (Do not test for
doneness; piercing the salt crust will
crack it and salt the interior of the
fish.)

MAKE THE <u>SALMORIGLIO</u> DRESSING:
While the fish is cooking, put the
olive oil in a mixing bowl. Add the
warm water and the lemon juice a little at a time, whisking continuously.
Add the remaining ingredients. Don't
be shy with the salt and pepper. Make
a double boiler by setting the bowl
over a simmering pan of water, and
whisk the mixture together for a few
minutes to warm it up.

Remove the fish from the oven. Crack
and remove the salt crust. Fillet and
portion the fish, topping each serving
with the dressing.

SERVES 8

Potato Salad with Celery Root, Walnuts, Gruyère, and Truffle Oil

1½ pounds Yukon Gold potatoes

1 pound celery root

½ pound Gruyère cheese, cut into matchsticks

1 cup coarsely chopped walnuts

1 teaspoon truffle oil

¼ cup extra virgin olive oil

½ teaspoon salt

Freshly ground black pepper to taste

Bring a pot of salted water to a boil. Boil the potatoes until fork tender, about 10 to 12 minutes, then drain them, peel them, and let them cool to room temperature. When cool, cut them into ½-inch-thick slices.

While the potatoes are cooling, peel the celery root and cut it into matchsticks (1½ by ¼ by ¼ inch). Blanch the celery root matchsticks for 1 minute in a pot of boiling salted water, then shock them in ice water for 1 minute. Drain and pat them dry.

Put the sliced potatoes in a bowl with the blanched and shocked celery matchsticks, along with the cheese and walnuts. Mix the truffle oil and the olive oil together, and drizzle the mixture over the salad. Season with the salt and toss thoroughly. Top with freshly ground black pepper.

SERVES 6 TO 8

Torta Sabbiosa

For the torta:

16 ounces butter, softened
16 ounces sugar
16 ounces potato starch
4 eggs
1 ounce baking powder
1 ounce Cognac
Vegetable oil cooking spray

For the sauce:

5 eggs, separated
5 tablespoons sugar
19 ounces mascarpone
1 ounce Cognac

MAKE THE TORTA: In a bowl, cream the butter and sugar together, then mix in the potato starch. Add the eggs, one at a time, mixing each one in completely before adding the next. Dissolve the baking powder in the Cognac and add it to the mixture.

Preheat the oven to 300°F. Line a 9 by 4 by 3-inch aluminum mold with parchment paper, spray the paper with vegetable oil, and fill the mold three quarters full with the batter. Bake in the preheated oven for 1 hour. Do not open the oven while the cake is baking!

MAKE THE SAUCE: In a bowl, beat the egg yolks with the sugar until creamy. Beat in the mascarpone and then the Cognac until they are well blended. Beat the egg whites until stiff, then fold them into the sauce.

Unmold the cake from the pan (it should come out easily thanks to the parchment paper), cut into 8 equal portions, plate each one separately, and top each serving with a generous spoonful of sauce.

SERVES 8

Chocolate and Amaretti Custard

8 eggs

⅜ cup unsweetened cocoa powder

1¼ cups sugar

½ cup finely chopped Amaretti di
  Saronno cookies

1 quart whole milk

½ cup water

To make the custard, you can use a processor, a mixer, an eggbeater, or a whisk. Beat the eggs together with the cocoa and ¾ cup of the sugar. Don't incorporate too much air—just beat them together. Add the crushed amaretti and beat to incorporate.

Last, add the milk and beat until homogenous.

Preheat the oven to 300°F. Put the remaining 1/2 cup of sugar in a skillet with the water. Bring it to a boil over high heat and cook until it reaches a medium-dark caramel color, 4 to 5 minutes. Pour the caramel into individual ramekins or a large savarin mold, making sure that it coats the surface evenly. Pour the custard into the mold(s), then set the mold(s) in a water bath, and bake in the preheated oven. If you're using individual molds, bake for 25 minutes; if you're using 1 large mold, bake for 1 hour. In either case, the top should be firm. Let the custard cool almost but not quite to room temperature before turning it out onto dessert plates or a platter.

SERVES 8

Christmas Day Lunch

Jerusalem Artichoke Salad
with Walnuts, Grapes, Pecorino, and Endive

1½ pounds Jerusalem artichokes
  (sunchokes)
1 large bowl filled with cold water and
  2 tablespoons lemon juice
4 Belgian endives
10 ounces pecorino Toscano cheese
½ teaspoon salt
Juice of 2 lemons
5 tablespoons extra virgin olive oil
2 cups walnut halves
10 ounces red grapes, halved and
  (if necessary) seeded
Freshly ground pepper to taste

Peel the Jerusalem artichokes and
slice them very thin, using a mandoline if you have one. Put the slices
in the acidulated water. Cut the
endives lengthwise into julienne
strips, then add them to the bowl. Cut
the cheese into julienne strips.

In a large salad bowl, dissolve the
salt in the fresh lemon juice by
whisking them together. Drizzle the
olive oil into the lemon juice, whisking continually to blend them well.

Drain the endives and Jerusalem artichokes and pat them dry. Add them,
along with the cheese, walnuts, and
grapes, to the salad bowl. Toss well
to coat all the ingredients with
dressing. Season with freshly ground
black pepper.

Serves 6

Tortellini in Capon Broth with Red Wine

For the dough:

2¾ cups "00" flour (see Note), or use
   all-purpose flour as a substitute

3 whole eggs

Egg wash: equal quantities egg yolk
   and water

For the broth:

1 capon (clean, ready to cook)

1 onion, peeled and rinsed

1 carrot, peeled and rinsed

1 stalk celery, peeled and rinsed

1 leek

Salt to taste

2 tablespoons dry red wine (optional)

For the tortellini:

3 ounces boneless pork (from the loin)

3 ounces boneless veal (from the loin)

3 ounces capon breast meat

2 tablespoons butter

Salt and freshly ground pepper
   to taste

3 ounces prosciutto

2 egg yolks

1 cup freshly grated Parmigiano-
   Reggiano, plus additional for serving

1 teaspoon grated nutmeg

NOTE: This high-gluten flour proofs extremely well. Purchase it in specialty stores or Italian markets.

MAKE THE DOUGH: On a clean work surface, mound the flour and make a well in the center. Place the eggs in the well and mix them into the flour a little at a time with the help of a fork. Then knead until the dough has a smooth and even consistency. Roll the dough out with a lightly floured rolling pin or run it through a pasta machine to make thin sheets about ⅛ inch thick.

MAKE THE CAPON BROTH: Place the capon in a large pot and fill with enough water to cover the capon. Add the vegetables and salt and bring to a boil. Lower the heat and simmer until the meat is tender, about 30 minutes per pound, skimming off the impurities that rise to the surface. Strain the broth through a fine strainer. Let it cool, then remove the fat that collects on the surface.

MAKE THE FILLING: Cut the pork, veal, and capon breast into 1-inch cubes. In a pan, melt the butter and sauté the cubes until they're golden brown. Season with salt and pepper.

Pass them twice through a meat grinder, and do the same with the prosciutto. Place all the ground meats in a bowl, and mix them with the egg yolks, cheese, and nutmeg; season again with salt and pepper. Mix until the filling is homogenous.

MAKE THE TORTELLINI: Cut each pasta sheet into 1¼-inch squares. Brush with the egg wash. Place ½ teaspoon of the filling in the middle of each square. Fold the dough into triangles, and seal, pressing down on the edges with your fingers. Fold the corners at the base of the triangle around your left index finger and press them firmly together between your right thumb and index finger. Place the tortellini on a floured tray, being careful they don't stick together.

To cook the pasta, bring the broth to a boil. Drop in the tortellini and cook them for 3 to 4 minutes after they float to the surface. If desired, add 2 tablespoons dry red wine (such as Lambrusco) to each bowl. Serve with grated cheese on the side.

SERVES 6

Capon Stuffed with Cotechino with Fruit Mustard and Green Sauce

For the capon:

One pound cotechino sausage

1½ pounds ground chicken breast

2 cups freshly grated Parmesan cheese

1 cup bread crumbs

3 eggs

½ cup shelled pistachios

¼ cup roughly chopped walnuts

¼ pound grapes

1 apple, peeled, cored, and cut into
  ¼-inch dice

Salt and freshly ground pepper to taste

1 carrot, peeled and cut into big pieces

1 stalk celery, cut into big pieces

1 onion, peeled and quartered

1 leek, carefully cleaned and cut into large pieces (including dark green parts)

For the green sauce:

1 cup fresh parsley leaves

3 tablespoons cornichons

1 tablespoon drained capers
3 tablespoons pickled onions
1 shallot, peeled
2 hard-boiled eggs, peeled
1 cup extra virgin olive oil
¾ cup red wine vinegar

To serve:

Mostardo di Frutta (mustard fruits,
    available at specialty stores and
    Italian markets)

MAKE THE CAPON: Place the
cotechino in a casserole filled with
cold water. Bring it to a boil, then
reduce the heat to low and simmer
slowly, partially covered, for 1 hour.
Remove from the liquid and let the
sausage cool to room temperature. Peel
off the skin. Set the cotechino aside.

In a bowl, mix the ground chicken,
Parmesan, bread crumbs, eggs, pistachios, walnuts, grapes, and apple
until they are well blended. Season
with salt and pepper. Cover the bottom
of the capon's cavity with a layer of
the stuffing. Place the peeled
cotechino on top of it, cutting off
the end if it doesn't fit inside the

cavity. Loosely fill the cavity with
the remainder of the stuffing. If all
of the stuffing doesn't fit loosely,
cook the balance in a buttered ovenproof dish. Seal the cavity by sewing
the skin around it shut with a needle
and string. Wrap the capon tightly in
a clean kitchen towel.

Put the carrot, celery, onion, and
leek in a big pot with salted water.
Bring the water to a boil, and add the
towel-wrapped capon. When the water
returns to a boil, reduce the heat and
simmer very slowly for 3 hours. Remove
the capon from the pot carefully and
place it on a cutting board to rest
for 30 minutes.

MAKE THE GREEN SAUCE: While the
bird cools, in a food processor, pulse
all the sauce ingredients until they
form a coarse mixture.

Remove the towel from the capon and
place the bird on a platter with
mostarda di frutta (available at
specialty and Italian stores) and
the green sauce.

SERVES 6

Spinach Flan with Glazed Carrots

2 cups whole milk

4 tablespoons unsalted butter, plus
   more for greasing

½ cup flour

½ teaspoon grated nutmeg

Salt and freshly ground pepper
   to taste

2 pounds fresh spinach, cleaned
   carefully, steamed, squeezed dry,
   and chopped fine

8 tablespoons freshly grated Parmesan
   cheese

8 eggs, separated

Glazed Carrots (recipe follows)

To make the béchamel, in a saucepan, warm the milk, but do not bring it to a boil. In a separate pan, melt the butter on low heat and add the flour, stirring continually with a whisk or wooden spoon until you have a golden brown roux, 3 to 4 minutes. Add the milk a little at a time, stirring continually to prevent lumps. When the milk is all in, continue cooking gently until the sauce thickens to the consistency of pastry cream, about 4 to 5 minutes more. Add the nutmeg and season with salt and pepper.

Preheat the oven to 300°F. Butter a non-stick flan mold (a ring shaped jello mold).

In a mixing bowl, combine the spinach with the béchamel, the cheese, and the egg yolks. Mix well. In a separate bowl, beat the egg whites with a pinch of salt until they are very stiff, then fold them into the spinach mixture with a rubber spatula. Season with salt and pepper. Pour the mixture into the flan mold and cook it in a water bath in the preheated oven for 1 hour, or until a toothpick inserted in the center of the flan comes out clean. Let the flan cool for 10 minutes, then turn it upside down onto a serving plate and fill the center with the glazed carrots.

SERVES 8

Glazed Carrots

4 tablespoons unsalted
   butter
1 pound medium-size
   carrots, peeled, cut in
   half lengthwise, steamed
   just until tender, and cut
   into ¼-inch slices
¼ cup milk
Pinch of ground cinnamon
Pinch of grated nutmeg
Salt and freshly ground
   pepper to taste
6 tablespoons freshly
   grated Parmesan
   cheese

In a saucepan over medium
heat, melt the butter.
Add the carrots and cook
for 5 minutes, until the
carrots are glistening.
Add the milk, cinnamon,
and nutmeg, season with
salt and pepper, and sim-
mer for 10 minutes more.
Stir in the Parmesan and
serve in the hole in the
center of the spinach
flan.

SERVES 8

Winter

Dried Fruit Filled with Cheese

1 tablespoon chopped walnuts, plus 8
  walnut halves
3 ounces mascarpone cheese
8 pitted prunes, soaked in warm water
  until moist (about 30 minutes) and
  then patted dry

3 ounces plain cream cheese
2 teaspoons candied ginger
1 teaspoon chopped lime zest
8 pitted dates
8 ½-inch cubes Gorgonzola cheese
8 dried figs, soaked in port until moist
  (about 1 hour), then patted dry and
  sliced almost entirely in half, leaving
  a "hinge" keeping the 2 halves
  attached

In a bowl, mix the chopped walnuts
with the mascarpone. Stuff the mixture
into the prunes. Top each prune with a
walnut half.

In a separate bowl, mix the cream
cheese with the candied ginger and
lime zest. Stuff the mixture into the
dates.

Put a Gorgonzola cube inside each fig,
then reclose the figs so that it looks
like the filling is bursting out of
them.

Arrange all of the stuffed fruits on a
serving platter.

SERVES 8

Compote with Blood Orange Sorbet

For the sorbet:

1¾ cups blood orange juice (8 to 10
   blood oranges)
4 tablespoons sugar (or slightly less,
   to taste)
1 tablespoon corn syrup

For the compote:

2 ruby red or pink grapefruits
2 blood oranges
3 navel oranges
1 lime
Sugar (optional)

MAKE THE SORBET: In a small
saucepan, warm (but do not boil) ½
cup of the blood orange juice with the
sugar and corn syrup until the sugar
is dissolved—the juice should feel
silky between your fingers. Pour the
warm mixture and the remaining juice
into the ice cream maker and follow
the manufacturer's instructions. Basically, you will want to freeze the
juice until it's slushy, stirring from
time to time, and then allow it to
set.

MAKE THE COMPOTE: Peel the fruit
over a bowl to catch as much juice as
possible as you cut away all of the
rind and pith. Cut into sections and
remove any seeds. Mix the fruit
together. Sweeten with a little sugar
if you wish.

Serve the compote over or next to the
sorbet.

SERVES

New Year's Eve Buffet
(Serves 30)

If the quintessential image of New Year's Eve in America is the ball falling in Times Square, then the quintessential image of New Year's in Tuscany is of old objects—plates, mirrors, even an occasional toilet—flying out of windows and crashing into bits on the street below. The Tuscan New Year's Eve tradition is to throw out all bad things in preparation for the coming year. In fact, the housewives of the region save their most memorable garbage just for this one night. In other words, New Year's Eve in Tuscany is a dangerous night to be out of doors.

Maybe it's for this reason that I gravitate toward staying indoors on New Year's Eve. Then again, maybe it's because I'm a restaurateur and find myself out almost every other night of the year. Whatever the reason, I enjoy being inside on New Year's Eve, and turning the evening into a gentle marathon of flavors with a buffet feast at which we can enjoy many different things.

For this special occasion, it's not a matter of "anything goes," it's "everything goes" in our kitchen. We take the energy most people put into getting crazy drunk and direct it toward our menu. Our buffet features appetizers as diverse as Turkey <u>Galantina</u> (below); Country Pâté in Crust (page 246), and a Leek Pudding with Foie Gras Sauce, Ginger, and Coriander (page 248).

There are two pastas, Tagliatelle Soufflé (page 252), a classic Tuscan dish representing the old, and, to represent the new, Crab Meat Ravioli in Ginger-Scented Vegetable Broth (page 254). Ginger is an unusual ingredient in Italian cooking, but for a night like this I find that its aroma lends the dish an extra elegance.

The centerpiece of the evening is an Oven-Baked Leg of Pork Glazed with Chestnut Honey (page 256), a rich, seasonal experience that should only be made and savored once a year.

And to end the evening memorably, there are two desserts, each of them rich in its own way: a Caramelized Baba Scented with Orange (page 260) and a Royal Chocolate Soup (page 262).

Too Much Food?" You'll notice that there are 9 dishes here, not including desserts, and that many of these recipes serve 8 to 12 people. This is because leftovers on this night are very intentional. See the New Year's Day Brunch (page 264) for more details.

NOTE: Even though many of these recipes only serve 8 to 12 people, if you make them all, you'll have more than enough to serve 30.

Turkey *Galantina*

10 medium asparagus

2½ pounds boneless turkey breast, in one piece, pounded into a large rectangle ¼ inch thick

4 ounces ground turkey breast

4 ounces ground pork loin

½ teaspoon salt

Freshly ground black pepper to taste

5 ounces ham (2 thick slices)

4 ounces boneless pork loin, cut into
long ½-inch-wide strips

8 cups chicken broth

Peel the bottom of the asparagus stems. Bring a pot of salted water to a boil and blanch the asparagus for a few minutes, then plunge them into ice water.

Place the pounded turkey on a cutting board. Mix the ground meats in a bowl and season with the salt and pepper. Spread a layer of ground meat $3/4$ inch thick on the turkey, leaving a $1^1/_4$-inch margin all around. Cover the ground meat with the ham. For the next layer, alternate asparagus and pork strips. Top with the remainder of the ground meat, spreading it evenly with a spatula. Roll the loaded turkey up tightly and wrap it in a clean kitchen towel. Tie the <u>galantina</u> firmly, as you would a roast, with one string lengthwise and several strings cross-wise.

In a pot, bring the broth to a boil. Place the <u>galantina</u> in a rectangular, lidded casserole (a fish poacher would be good) and pour the boiling broth over it. Simmer on low heat, covered, for 2 hours. Let the <u>galantina</u> cool down to room temperature in the broth, then remove it from the broth and put it under a 2-pound weight for 6 hours. Refrigerate it overnight. It should be firm and shiny. Don't forget to take off the towel before serving!

SERVES 12 TO 15

Country Pâté in Crust

1 pound boneless loin of veal

3 ounces fatback, sliced ⅛ inch thick

4 ounces ham, in 1 thick slice

1 tablespoon Cognac

1 pound boneless loin of pork

1 pound loose sweet Italian sausage
   meat

½ cup bread crumbs

2 whole eggs, plus 1 egg yolk

½ teaspoon salt

Freshly ground black pepper to taste

1 pound frozen puff pastry, rolled out

2 tablespoons chopped fresh Italian
   parsley

6 tablespoons prepared cold gelatin,
   made following instructions on box of
   powdered gelatin

NOTE: If you prefer, you may buy ½ pound of the veal and pork already ground, but be sure to buy an additional ¼ pound of each uncut.

Preheat the oven to 300° F. Cut ¼ pound of the veal loin, the fatback, and the ham, into 1½-inch-wide strips. Put the strips on a plate and sprinkle the Cognac over them. Grind (see Note) the remaining veal loin and the pork loin, then combine them in a bowl with the sausage meat, bread crumbs, whole eggs, salt, and a few grindings of pepper.

Line an ovenproof pâté mold (preferably with removable sides) with the puff pastry, making sure to reserve enough pastry to cover the top. Alternate layers of ground meat and strips, sprinkling a little of the chopped parsley between each layer. Top with the reserved puff pastry, sealing it to the pastry lining the mold by pinching them together. Make a ¼-inch round hole in the top crust with a knife. Make an egg wash by mixing the egg yolk with half an eggshell full of water. Brush the egg wash on the top crust, then bake the pâté in the preheated oven for 2 hours. If the crust gets too brown, cover it with foil. If you are using a mold with removable sides, open up the mold and take the sides off when the 2 hours have elapsed; brush the sides with egg wash, and bake for 10 minutes more. If you are not using a mold with removable sides, just leave the pâté in the mold and bake for the additional 10 minutes.

Remove the pâté from the oven and let it cool down to room temperature. Pour the cold gelatin into the pâté through the hole in the crust. Chill in the refrigerator for about half an hour to set the gelatin. Slice to serve.

SERVES 12 TO 15

Leek Pudding
with Foie Gras Sauce, Ginger, and Coriander

For the pudding:

2 pounds whole leeks

4 tablespoons butter

¼ cup extra virgin olive oil

1 cup chicken stock, as needed

4 egg yolks

1 cup freshly grated Parmesan
    cheese

¼ teaspoon grated nutmeg

Salt and freshly ground pepper
    to taste

Vegetable oil cooking spray, such as
    Pam, for greasing the ramekins

For the sauce:

32 coriander seeds, or 1 tablespoon
    ground coriander

1 tablespoon grated fresh ginger

1 cup white wine

1 cup chicken stock

7 ounces fresh raw foie gras, cut into
    ½-inch dice

Salt and freshly ground pepper
    to taste

1 tablespoon chopped fresh Italian
    parsley

MAKE THE PUDDING: Wash the leeks carefully, then slice the white and light green parts very thin. In a heavy saucepan or casserole with a lid, warm the butter and the olive oil over very low heat. Add the sliced leeks and cook, covered, until they are falling apart into a puree, about 1 hour, adding broth if they stick to the bottom of the pan. Remove them from the heat, scrape them into a mixing bowl, and let them cool to room temperature.

Preheat the oven to 300°F. Spray 8 individual ramekins with the vegetable oil spray.

Beat the egg yolks, Parmesan, nutmeg, and salt and pepper into the leeks with a whisk. Then pour the leek puree into the ramekins. Make a water bath by placing the molds in a pan filled with 1/2 inch of water, and bake in the preheated oven until the tops are golden and firm, about 25 minutes.

MAKE THE SAUCE: Grind the coriander seeds and add them to a sauté pan with the grated ginger and wine. Bring to a boil over high heat, then reduce the heat to medium and cook until the alcohol has evaporated, 3 to 4 minutes. Add the stock and cook for 5 minutes more. Add the diced foie gras and cook for another 5 minutes. Pass the mixture through a food mill, using the disk with the smallest holes, then return the sauce to the pan and bring it back to a boil. Season with salt and pepper and stir in the parsley. Remove from the heat.

Turn the puddings upside down onto individual plates (use a knife to edge them out if necessary) and coat them with the sauce.

SERVES 10

Pan Brioche Scented with Fennel

4 tablespoons butter

1½ cups milk

1 envelope dry yeast

4 cups "00" flour (see Note),
   or all-purpose if not available, plus
   additional for coating work surface
   and pan

2 eggs

1 teaspoon salt

2 teaspoons fennel seeds

NOTE: This high-gluten flour proofs extremely well. Purchase it at specialty stores or Italian markets.

In a pan, melt half the butter over low heat. In another pan, warm the milk slightly over low heat and dissolve the yeast in it. Place some flour on a clean work surface and mound the 4 cups on this. Make a well in the center. Put the melted butter, 1 whole egg, the yeast mixture, and the salt in the center of the well.

Knead the dough for about 10 minutes, until it's smooth and elastic. Place it in a bowl, cover with plastic wrap, and set it in a warm place to rise for about 1 hour. Then, knead the dough again for about 5 minutes and place it in a loaf pan greased with the remaining butter and dusted with flour. Cover with plastic and let it rise for 2 hours.

Preheat the oven to 300°F.

Combine the remaining egg yolk with an equal quantity of water. Brush the top of the loaf with the egg wash and sprinkle it with fennel seeds. Bake it in the preheated oven for about 1 hour, or until a toothpick inserted in the center comes out dry. Let cool upside down until the brioche drops out when the mold is lifted.

MAKES 1 LOAF

Tagliatelle Soufflé

For the béchamel:

6 tablespoons butter
⅓ cup flour
4 cups hot milk
½ teaspoon grated nutmeg
Salt and freshly ground pepper
   to taste

For the soufflé:

¾ cup freshly grated Parmesan cheese
1 cup freshly grated Emmenthaler
   cheese
4 egg yolks
13 ounces dry tagliatelle (flat, narrow
   egg noodles—if you use fresh, you'll
   need 1 pound)
6 tablespoons butter, room temperature
6 egg whites

MAKE THE BÉCHAMEL: In a saucepan over medium-low heat, melt the butter. Add the flour and stir constantly until the roux turns golden brown, about 3 minutes. Add the milk, a little at a time, stirring constantly to prevent lumps. Cook until the sauce thickens, about 5 minutes. Remove from the heat, stir in the nutmeg, and season with salt and pepper.

MAKE THE SOUFFLÉ: Stir the grated cheeses into the béchamel while it's still hot, but off the heat. When the sauce is no longer hot, but still warm, mix in the egg yolks, one at a time. In a large pot of boiling salted water, blanch the tagliatelle for just a couple of minutes—they will cook more in the oven. Drain the pasta, but reserve 5 tablespoons of the water in which they were cooked. In a large mixing bowl, toss the tagliatelle with 4 tablespoons of the butter and the reserved pasta water. Add the béchamel to the pasta, stirring all the while to mix everything thoroughly. Let the mixture cool to room temperature, mix-

ing once in a while to prevent settling, separation, and sticking.

While the pasta is cooling, preheat the oven to 375°F. Use the remaining 2 tablespoons of butter to grease a 3-quart soufflé dish. In a bowl, whip the egg whites to stiff peaks. When the pasta has cooled down, stir the beaten egg whites carefully into the soufflé mixture. Add the soufflé mixture to the soufflé dish, evening the surface with a spatula. Bake in the preheated oven for 30 minutes. Reduce the heat to 350° and cook for 10 minutes more. Do not open the oven while the soufflé is cooking—if you do, it is likely to fall. When the soufflé has "puffed" up about 1 to 2 inches over the top of the dish, remove it from the oven gently and bring it to the table immediately to serve.

SERVES 8 TO 10

Crab Meat Ravioli
in Ginger-Scented Vegetable Broth

For the pasta:

4 cups "00" flour (see Note), or use
   all-purpose flour as a substitute
5 eggs, plus 1 egg yolk

For the filling:

1 pound fresh crab meat, picked
   through, excess water squeezed out
1 cup ricotta cheese
½ cup freshly grated Parmesan cheese
1 egg
1 tablespoon chopped fresh chives
½ teaspoon salt
Freshly ground black pepper to taste

For the broth:

2 carrots, peeled and cut into big
   pieces
2 stalks celery, trimmed and cut into
   big pieces
1 leek, carefully washed and cut into
   big pieces
10 cups cold water
Salt to taste
5 ounces fresh ginger

NOTE: This high-gluten flour proofs extremely well. Purchase it in specialty stores or Italian markets.

MAKE THE PASTA: On a clean, smooth work surface, mound the flour and make a well in the center. Add the 5 whole eggs and mix the flour into the center with a fork, a little at a time, until all the flour has been absorbed. Knead with your hands until the dough has a smooth and even consistency. Pass the dough through the pasta machine as many times as necessary to obtain a very thin sheet (less than 1/8 inch). Repeat until all the dough has been converted into sheets.

MAKE THE FILLING: In a bowl, mix all the filling ingredients together until they are well blended.

MAKE THE RAVIOLI: Spread half the pasta sheets out on a clean working surface. Place small dollops (1/2 teaspoon) of filling at 1½-inch intervals on the pasta until the filling has been used up. Make an egg wash by mixing the egg yolk with half an eggshell full of water. Brush the egg wash around the mounds of filling. Cover with the remaining pasta sheets, pressing with your fingers around the filling to eliminate air and to seal the ravioli. Cut the sheets into square ravioli with a cutting wheel. Place the ravioli on a floured tray.

MAKE THE BROTH: Place the vegetables in a pot with the cold water. If the vegetables are not covered, add more water to cover. Bring the water to a boil, then reduce the heat and simmer for 30 minutes. Season with salt. Extract the juice from the ginger using a juice extractor (if you don't have a juice extractor, smash the ginger to a pulp with a meat pounder or mallet, place the pulp in a clean towel, and twist the towel to squeeze the juice out). Add the juice to the broth (use less if you don't like too much ginger). Pour the broth through a strainer, then bring it back to a boil. Drop the ravioli into the boiling broth and cook them for 2 minutes after they float. Serve in bowls with the broth.

SERVES 10 TO 12

Oven-Baked Leg of Pork Glazed
with Chestnut Honey

1 bone-in leg of pork, about 12 pounds
Salt and freshly ground pepper
   to taste
3 leeks, white and light green parts
   only, washed carefully and cut into
   ½-inch slices
3 large carrots, peeled and cut into
   ½-inch slices
2 sprigs fresh rosemary
2 sprigs fresh sage
4 sprigs fresh thyme
1 cup extra virgin olive oil
4 tablespoons butter
1 bottle dry champagne
1 cup chestnut honey*

Preheat the oven to 300° F. Rub the pork with plenty of salt and some pepper. Strew the vegetables and fresh herbs all over a large roasting pan, then drizzle the olive oil over them. Place the leg of pork on top, and dot it with the butter. Cover with foil and bake in the preheated oven for 1½ hours. Then pour the champagne over the pork, cover it again, and put it back in the oven. After another 1½ hours, take it out and brush it with the chestnut honey. This time, leave the foil off, turn the heat up to 450°, and put the pork back in the oven for another 1½ hours, basting it every 30 minutes. By now, the pork should have a shiny golden crust.

Remove the pork leg to a channeled carving board. Skim the fat from the roasting pan, then pass the remaining juices, vegetables, and herbs included, through a food mill. Season the sauce to taste with salt and pepper, and serve it on the side. Carve the leg at the table, only taking off as much as is being served.

S E R V E S   1 5

*Available at upscale
gourmet shops.

Caramelized Onions and Chestnuts

30 Italian cipolline onions, peeled
20 frozen chestnuts
6 tablespoons unsalted butter
Salt and freshly ground pepper
   to taste
4 tablespoons dark brown sugar
1 cup vegetable broth

Bring a pot of salted water to a boil. Blanch the cipolline and chestnuts for 3 minutes, then drain them and spread them out on a sheet pan to cool.

In a sauté pan over medium heat, melt the butter then stir in the cipolline. When they are all coated, stir in the chestnuts. Season with salt and pepper, and add the brown sugar. Continue cooking until the sugar caramelizes, 3 to 4 minutes, then add the broth, reduce the heat to low, and continue cooking until the liquid is reduced to a syrupy consistency, 15 to 20 minutes. Serve hot.

SERVES 10 TO 12

Carrot and Apple Puree

1½ pounds carrots, peeled and cut into
 ½-inch dice
1½ pounds potatoes, peeled and cut
 into ½-inch dice
1 pound apples, preferably Golden
 Delicious
Grated zest of 1 orange
10 tablespoons butter, softened to room
 temperature
1 cup freshly grated Parmesan cheese
¼ cup heavy cream
½ teaspoon grated nutmeg
½ teaspoon ground cinnamon
Salt and freshly ground pepper
 to taste

Preheat the oven to 300°F. Bring a
pot of lightly salted water to a boil,
add the carrots, and cook for 5 minutes, then add the potatoes and cook
until tender, another 7 to 10 minutes.
Meanwhile, peel and core the apples,
then wrap them individually in foil
and bake them in the preheated oven
until they're soft, about 30 minutes.
Drain the carrots and potatoes, unwrap
the baked apples, and pass all through
a food mill or ricer. Put the mashed
carrots, potatoes, and apples in a
large mixing bowl, and whisk in all
the remaining ingredients except the
salt and pepper to obtain a fluffy,
smooth puree. Season with salt and
pepper.

SERVES 10 TO 12

Caramelized Baba Scented with Orange

For the baba:

¹/₂ ounce dry yeast

2 tablespoons warm water

¹/₄ cup warm milk

1 cup all-purpose flour, plus more for
dusting the pan

1 teaspoon salt

2 eggs

1 tablespoon sugar

8 tablespoons butter, diced, at room
temperature, plus more for greasing
the pan

**For the oranges and
caramel:**

8 oranges

²/₃ cup brewed tea

1 cup sugar

¹/₄ cup kirsch (you can
substitute rum)

¹/₄ cup water

MAKE THE DOUGH: In a
large mixing bowl, mix
the yeast with the warm
water, 1 tablespoon of
the warm milk, the flour,
and the salt. Mix in the
eggs one at a time. Knead
the dough for 7 minutes,
until it is smooth and
elastic. (You can do this
in a processor by puls-
ing.) Knead in the rest
of the milk, then the
sugar, and last, the but-

ter. Cover the dough with a towel and set it in a warm place to rise for 30 minutes.

Preheat the oven to 375°F. Grease a 7-inch savarin mold with butter and then dust it with flour. Transfer the dough to the savarin mold and let it rise again for 30 minutes more, by which time the dough should have risen nearly to the rim. Put the savarin in the preheated oven and bake for 25 minutes, or until the top is golden and a toothpick inserted in the center comes out clean.

MAKE THE ORANGES AND CARAMEL:
In a small saucepan, squeeze the juice from 3 of the oranges and add it to the tea along with half the sugar and half of the kirsch. Bring the mixture to a boil on low heat, and cook until the mixture caramelizes to a golden brown and thickens into a syrup, 15 to 20 minutes. While the mixture is simmering, peel the remaining oranges, section them, and peel the membrane from each section with a sharp paring knife. In a separate saucepan over low heat, dissolve the remaining sugar with the remaining kirsch and the water. When the sugar has dissolved, remove it from the heat and let it cool. When it reaches room temperature, add the peeled orange segments and let them soak for at least half an hour.

When the baba is done, remove it from the oven and turn it out onto a serving platter. Drizzle the caramelized syrup all over it. Lift the orange segments from their soaking liquid and place them in the hole in the center of the baba, then drizzle the soaking liquid over the baba.

SERVES 12

Royal Chocolate "Soup"

This is more like a pudding than a soup, but it "eats" like a soup due to its delicate nature. In Italy, this dish is called <u>Zuppa Reale al Cioccolato.</u>

10 ounces semisweet chocolate
8 tablespoons unsalted butter
4 tablespoons sugar
4 tablespoons water
8 eggs, separated
76 ladyfingers
1 cup brewed espresso
Shaved chocolate, for garnish

In a metal mixing bowl, place the chocolate, butter, sugar, and water. Make a double boiler by putting the bowl over a small pan of simmering water. Melt the ingredients, beating continually, to form a cream. Remove from the heat, let the chocolate cool for just 5 minutes, then add the egg yolks gradually, beating continually. In a bowl, whip the egg whites to stiff peaks and fold them into the cream, which should be room temperature by this point. Chill the chocolate cream in the refrigerator for 15 minutes.

Line the bottom of a 10-inch cake pan with parchment paper. Cover the parchment paper with a layer of ladyfingers dipped for just a second or two in espresso. Line the sides of the pan with undipped ladyfingers, cutting them so that their height does not exceed that of the cake pan. Reserve 4 tablespoons of the chocolate cream to spread over the cake. Spread the remainder between layers of ladyfingers dipped for 3 or 4 seconds in espresso. When the pan is full of alternating layers of espresso-dipped ladyfingers and chocolate cream, refrigerate it overnight. The next day, turn it out onto a platter. Spread the reserved chocolate cream thinly all over the cake, and decorate it with the shaved chocolate.

S E R V E S   1 0   T O   1 2

New Year's Day Brunch

(Serves 6)

New Year's Day offers a chance to explore one of the essential components of Tuscan cooking—using leftovers the day after a big meal. Not only is this subtle art at the heart of our culture, but it's especially appropriate to a New Year's Day feast because it allows one meal to straddle two years.

Some examples of using leftovers here are taking the remaining Tagliatelle Soufflé (page 252) and making Golden Tagliatelle Fritters (page 266); using the remaining Oven-Baked Leg of Pork Glazed with Chestnut Honey (page 256) in a Sliced Leg of Pork Gratiné with Truffle Paste and Fontina Cheese (page 267); and the leftover Turkey Galantina (page 244) in a Turkey Salad with Haricots Verts (page 265).

Pay attention to the techniques that allow these dishes to be reused; you can apply them to a number of different contexts.

But the one essential dish on New Year's Day is not made from leftovers. It's the Cotechino with Lentils (page 268), a pork-filled sausage with lentils and sabayon flavored with balsamic vinegar. Not only is this dish a tradition on New Year's Day; it's actually bad luck not to have it. If you've found bad luck in your life over the last few years, try starting the new year with this recipe and see if it helps.

Turkey Salad with Haricots Verts

4 slices Turkey <u>Galantina</u> (page 244), each ¼ inch thick

8 ounces haricots verts, trimmed and blanched for 3 minutes in salted water, then shocked in ice water and drained

1 Granny Smith apple, cored, halved, and cut lengthwise into ⅛-inch slices

½ cup coarsely chopped walnuts

½ teaspoon salt

2 tablespoons Aspretto* or raspberry vinegar

4 tablespoons extra virgin olive oil

Freshly ground black pepper to taste

Cut the turkey <u>galantina</u> slices into ¼-inch strips. Mix them in a bowl with the haricots verts, sliced apple, and walnuts. Dissolve the salt in the vinegar with a whisk. Add the olive oil to the vinegar, continuing to whisk until emulsified. Pour the vinaigrette over the salad and toss thoroughly. Grind pepper over the salad.

SERVES 6

*This Italian import is available in upscale gourmet and specialty shops.

Golden Tagliatelle Fritters

Leftover Tagliatelle Soufflé (page 252)
1 cup flour
2 eggs, beaten and seasoned with
    ½ teaspoon salt
2 cups bread crumbs
1 quart vegetable oil, for frying
Salt to taste

Divide the tagliatelle leftovers into
½-cup portions. Shape each portion
into a plump hamburger and squeeze it
tightly to help it hold its shape. On
your counter, leading up to a sheet
pan lined with wax paper, arrange a
plate with the flour, a bowl with the
eggs, and a plate with the bread
crumbs. Roll each fritter in the
flour, dip it in the egg, then roll it

in the bread crumbs. Set the prepared
fritters on the wax paper-lined sheet
pan.

In a deep pan over medium-high heat,
warm the oil until it reaches 375°F.
(a drop of water will crackle and
splutter). Fry the fritters in small
batches until golden brown, about 5
minutes on each side. Do not crowd the
pan or the oil will not stay hot
enough. As each batch is ready, lift
it from the pan with a slotted spoon
or a skimmer onto a plate lined with
paper towels. Season with salt and
serve very hot.

SERVES 6

Sliced Leg of Pork Gratiné
with Truffle Paste and Fontina

2 tablespoons unsalted butter

¼ cup flour

3½ cups chicken stock, kept at a
simmer

1 ounce dried porcini mushrooms,
soaked in water for 1 hour, then
drained, squeezed dry, and chopped
fine

18 slices leftover oven-baked leg of
pork (page 256)

4½ teaspoons truffle paste

18 thin slices fontina Val D'Aosta
cheese

18 thin slices ham

In a large, heavy-bottomed saucepan or casserole over low heat, melt the butter. Add the flour and mix vigorously with a wooden spoon until it forms a smooth, golden paste. Add half of the simmering stock in a thin stream, whisking constantly to avoid lumps. When the sauce comes to a boil, add the remaining stock and the chopped mushrooms. Simmer for 10 minutes more, stirring frequently. This is a velouté sauce.

Preheat the oven to 375°F. Spread each slice of meat with ¼ teaspoon of the truffle paste. Cover each slice with a slice of fontina and then a slice of ham. Arrange the layered slices in an ovenproof gratin dish (usually oval and porcelain) so that the slices overlap. Pour the velouté sauce over the slices. Bake in the preheated oven for 20 to 30 minutes, or until the cheese is completely melted. Bring the whole gratin dish to the table to serve.

S E R V E S   6

Cotechino with Lentils

2 cotechino sausages, 1 pound each
8 ounces dry green lentils, picked
   clean and rinsed
1 tablespoon salt, plus extra to taste
¼ cup extra virgin olive oil
3 tablespoons finely chopped onion
2 tablespoons finely chopped carrot
2 tablespoons finely chopped celery
½ cup Basic Tomato Sauce
   (page 93)
Freshly ground pepper to taste
8 egg yolks
3 tablespoons sugar
2 tablespoons traditional balsamic
   vinegar (see Note)

*NOTE: Use only authentic Aceto Bal-
samico Tradizionale di Modena.*

In a pot that will fit them both horizontally (a fish poacher should work
well), cover the cotechino sausages
with cold water. Bring the water to a
boil over high heat, then reduce the
heat to low and simmer, covered, until
a thermometer inserted in the center
of a sausage reads 160°F., about 1
hour.

While the cotechino sausages are simmering, in a deep saucepan, cover the

lentils with cold water and a tablespoon of salt. Bring to a boil over
high heat, then reduce the heat and
simmer, partially covered, until the
lentils are cooked through, about 30
minutes, skimming the foam that collects on the surface from time to
time. When the lentils are cooked,
drain them of all but 1/2 cup of their
cooking liquid and set them aside.

While the lentils are simmering, in a
large skillet over medium heat, warm
the olive oil. Add the chopped onion,
carrot, and celery, and cook until
they are soft, about 10 minutes. Stir
in the drained lentils with their
reserved cooking liquid and cook for 5
minutes. Add the tomato sauce and cook
for 10 minutes more. Season with salt
and pepper.

MAKE THE ZABAGLIONE: In a large
metal mixing bowl set over a pot of
simmering water, beat the egg yolks
and sugar together with a whisk until
they are foamy, 3 to 5 minutes. Take
the bowl out of the simmering water
and beat in the balsamic vinegar.

Serve the cotechino and lentils on a
platter, with the zabaglione on the
side, to pour over the slices of
cotechino.

SERVES 6

Chocolate Pudding with Caramelized Pear

For the pudding:

3½ ounces semisweet chocolate
2 tablespoons unsalted butter
4 tablespoons unsweetened cocoa
   powder
2 tablespoons flour
3 tablespoons potato starch
5 tablespoons sugar
4 cups whole milk
¼ cup brandy

For the caramelized pears:

8 to 10 pears (1 per person), peeled
   but left whole
2½ quarts water
7 cups sugar
One 3-inch cinnamon stick
2 whole cloves

MAKE THE PUDDING: Cut the chocolate into small chunks. In a bowl set
over a pan of simmering water, melt
the chunks with the butter. When the
mixture is creamy, remove the bowl
from the pan. In a saucepan off the
heat, combine the cocoa, flour, potato

continued

Winter

starch, and sugar. Add a small amount of the milk to make a paste, then add the rest of the milk in a stream, beating continually, until everything is dissolved and the mixture is free of lumps. Add the melted chocolate to the pan and warm the pudding over very low heat, stirring very frequently, until the mixture thickens to the consistency of pastry cream, about 15 minutes. Remove the pan from the heat, stir in the brandy, and let the pudding cool to room temperature, mixing occasionally. Refrigerate until it sets, at least 3 hours or even overnight if it's more convenient for you.

MAKE THE PEARS: Place the pears in a casserole with the water, sugar, cinnamon, and cloves. Bring the liquid to a boil, then reduce the heat to low, cover, and simmer for about 20 minutes, or until the pears are cooked through but still firm enough to handle without breaking apart. Remove the pears with a slotted spoon and set them aside. Turn the heat up to medium-high and cook the liquid until it reduces to a caramelized syrup, about 15 minutes. Remove the cinnamon stick and the cloves. Put the pears back in the casserole and coat them with the caramelized syrup.

Serve a scoop of pudding with a glazed pear on the side, and some syrup drizzled over it.

SERVES 8 TO 10

Valentine's Day

(Serves 2)

I can't think of a day on which I would like to cook less than on Valentine's Day. But if you are in the mood to do so, my advice is to keep it simple and light—or short and sweet—leaving yourself time and energy to spend with your valentine.

My approach to Valentine's Day involves mostly seafood, starting with an Artichoke Heart Salad with Oysters and Radicchio (page 276) and a Monkfish and Fennel Consommé (page 279), delicious dishes that are big on flavor but not too filling.

For the pasta and main course,

I have provided recipes for Spaghetti with Lobster, Tomato, and Basil (page 281) and Baked Salmon with King Crab and Black Truffle Mashed Potatoes (page 282). Both these dishes are dramatic and indulgent, packed with sensuous flavors and textures, which are very appropriate to the occasion.

For dessert, there is a sort of edible frozen after-dinner drink, the Vin Santo Gelatin with Grapes (page 284). Toast yourselves for having found love, and let this warm your souls on a cold winter night as you look forward to spring together.

XXL
A Silvia

Silvia, rimembri ancora
Quel tempo della tue vita mortale
Quando beltà splendea
Negli occhi tuoi ridenti e fuggitivi,
E tu, lieta e pensoso, il limitare
Di gioventù salivi?

To Silvia

Silvia, do you still remember
The time in your brief life here
When beauty brightened
Your eyes and your shy smile,
And you stood in pensive joy on the brink
Of becoming a young woman?

Sonavan le quiete
Stanze, e le vie dintorno,
Al tuo perpetuo canto,
Allor che all'opre femminili intenta
Sedevi, assai contenta
Di quel vago avvenir che in mente aevi.
Era il maggio adoroso: e tu solevi
Così menare il giorno

Io gli studi leggiadri
Talor lasciando e le sudate carte,
Ove il tempo mio primo
E di me si spendea la miglior,
parte,
D'in si i veroni del paterno ostello
Porgea gli orecchi al suon della tua voce,
Ed alla man veloce
Che per correa la faticosa tela.
Mirava il ciel sereno,
Le vie dorate e gli orti,
E quinci il mar da lungi, e quindi il monte.
Lingua mortal non dice
Quel ch'io sentiva in seno.

Che pensieri soavi,
Che speranze, che cori, o Silvia mia!
Quale allor ci apparia
La vita umana e il fato!
Quando sovviemmi di cotanta speme,
Un affetto mi preme
Acerbo e sconsolato,
E tornami a doler di mia sventura

All day the hushed rooms
And the roads around the house
Rang with your singing
As you bent to the spinning wheel,
Happily adrift in your hazy
Dreams of the future. Day
After day you spent like that,
All the fragrant month of May.

Sometimes, getting up
From the books I loved
And those sweat-stained pages
Where I spent the best of my youth,
I'd lean from the terrace of my father's house
Toward the sound of your voice
And the quick click of your hands
At the heavy loom. Wonder-struck, I'd stare
Up at the cloudless blue of the sky,
Out at the kitchen gardens and the roads
That shone like gold, and off there
To the mountains and, there, to the distant sea.
No human tongue could tell
The feelings beating in my heart.

What tender thoughts we had,
What hopes, what hearts, Silvia!
How fate and human life
Looked then! Now
When I think of all that hope
I'm bitterly stricken,
Beyond consolation, and begin
Lamenting again my own misfortunes.

Olio di Oliva

O natura, o natura.
Perchè non rendi poi
Quel che prometti allor? perchè di tanto
Inganni i figli tuoi?

Tu pria che l'erbe inaridisse il verno,
Da chiuso morbo combattuta e vinta,
Perivi, o tenerella. E non vedevi
Il fio degli anni tuoi;
Non ti molceva il core
La dolce lode or delle negre chiome,
Or degli sguardi innamorati e schivi;
Nè teco le compagne ai dì festivi
Ragionavan d'amore.

Anche peria fra poco
La speranza mia dolce: agli anni miei
Anche negaro I fati
La giovanezza. Ahi come,
Come passata sei,
Cara compagna dell'età mio nova,
Mia lacrimata speme!
Questo è quel mondo? questi
I diletti, l'amor, l'opre, gli eventi
Onde contanto ragionamo insieme?
Questa la sorte dell'umane genti?
All'apparir del vero
Tu, misera, cadesti: e con la mano
La fredda morte ed una tomba ignuda
Mostravi di lontano.

—GIACOMO LEOPARDI

Ah, nature, nature, why
Can you never make good
Your promises? Why
Must you so deceive your own children?

Before winter had withered the grass,
You were dying, dear girl,
Struck and cut down by blind disease.
And you didn't see your years
Break into blossom, nor ever felt
Your heart melt
Under honeyed praise of your jet-black tresses
Or the shy enamored light in your eyes.
And never did your friends spend Sundays
Whispering with you, all about love.

And soon, too, my own fond hopes
Withered and died: my youth, too,
The fates cut off. Ah,
Alas how you've faded,
My tearstained hope, belovèd
Comrade of those spring days!
Is this the world we imagined? These
The pleasures, love, adventures
We two together talked and talked of?
Is this what it means to be born human?
At the very first touch of things as they are
You shriveled, poor thing,
And with raised hand pointed away
To the cold figure of death
And an unmarked grave.

—translated by
EAMON GRENNAN

Artichoke Heart Salad with
Oysters and Radicchio

8 fresh oysters

6 baby artichokes

Juice of 1 lemon

½ pound radicchio trevigiano
   (see Note)

1 clove garlic, finely chopped

½ teaspoon salt, plus extra to taste

⅓ cup extra virgin olive oil

Freshly ground black pepper to taste

NOTE: Radicchio trevigiano, a long-leaved variety of radicchio, is available at Italian markets and grocers with gourmet produce sections.

Shuck the oysters and save their liquor, filtering it through a double thickness of cheesecloth. Remove the tough outer leaves from the artichokes; trim the tips and stems. Place the trimmed artichokes in a pot of water acidulated with half the lemon juice, and steam them for approximately 10 minutes, until cooked but still firm. Cool them to room temperature and set aside.

Rinse and spin dry the radicchio, then cut into julienne strips.

Place the garlic in a bowl with the ½ teaspoon of salt. Using a whisk to combine, add 3 teaspoons of lemon juice and the liquor from the oysters. Then add the olive oil, continuing to whisk until the dressing is emulsified.

Reserve 2 tablespoons of dressing. Toss the oysters and radicchio in a bowl with the remaining dressing, then place it in the center of a serving platter. Arrange the artichokes, cut in half (cut side facing up) all around the oysters and on top of them. Season with salt and pepper. Drizzle the artichokes with the reserved dressing.

SERVES 2

Monkfish and Fennel Consommé

For the fish broth:

1½ pounds fish bones (from white-
  fleshed, as opposed to oily fish),
  rinsed
1 leek, white and green parts, carefully
  cleaned and cut into big pieces
1 stalk celery, cut into big pieces
5 mushrooms (caps only if the stems
  are dirty)
3 sprigs fresh thyme
1 bay leaf
10 sprigs fresh Italian parsley
5 cups cold water
Salt and freshly ground pepper
  to taste

For the consommé:

7 ounces monkfish fillet, skin removed
7 ounces bulb fennel, plus fennel fronds
  for garnish
¼ cup olive oil
2 cups water
Salt and freshly ground pepper
  to taste

MAKE THE BROTH: Place all the broth ingredients except the salt and pepper in a deep saucepan. There should be enough water to cover the solids. If not, add enough additional water to cover. Bring the liquid to a boil over high heat, then reduce the heat and simmer, covered, for 30 minutes, skimming the foam frequently. Pour the broth through a fine mesh sieve or strainer. Season with salt and pepper.

MAKE THE CONSOMMÉ: While the broth is cooking, slice the monkfish as thinly and broadly as you can. Remove and discard the toughest outer fennel layer and slice what's left lengthwise, again very thin. In a sauté pan over medium heat warm the olive oil. Add the fennel and cook for 2 minutes. Add the water, bring it to a boil, reduce the heat to medium, and cook for 3 minutes, until the fennel is just cooked. Drain the fennel and season it with salt and pepper.

Arrange the sliced fish and the fennel in 2 bowls. Pour the piping hot fish broth on top. (The hot broth will cook the thinly sliced fish, so be sure the broth is as hot as indicated in these directions.) Garnish each bowl with a fennel frond.

SERVES 2

Spaghetti with Lobster, Tomato, and Basil

½ cup extra virgin olive oil

2 whole cloves garlic, peeled

1 live lobster, 1½ pounds

½ cup white wine

1 pound ripe tomatoes

10 leaves fresh basil, torn roughly by
    hand

Pinch of hot red pepper flakes

2 tablespoons chopped fresh Italian
    parsley leaves

Salt and freshly ground pepper
    to taste

12 ounces dry spaghetti

Reserve 3 tablespoons of olive oil for later use. In a sauté pan over medium-high heat, warm the remaining oil. Add the garlic and sauté until it is golden brown all over, 2 to 3 minutes. Cut the lobster in half lengthwise with a big cleaver and add to the pan cut side down. Sauté until the lobster meat that shows is golden, about 5 minutes. Reduce the heat to medium, pour the wine over the lobster, and continue cooking until the liquid has evaporated.

While the wine is evaporating, in a large pot of boiling water, blanch the tomatoes for 2 minutes, then plunge them into ice water. Peel the tomatoes, halve them horizontally, and remove the seeds. Dice the seeded tomatoes into ½-inch cubes, then stir them into the pan with the lobsters, along with the basil and hot red pepper. Cook for 10 minutes, then take the pan off the heat. Remove the lobsters, extract the meat from the shells, and cut it into small chunks. Return the meat to the sauce. Add the parsley and season with salt and pepper. Simmer for 5 minutes more.

In a large pot of boiling lightly salted water, cook the spaghetti until it is al dente. Drain the spaghetti and add it to the sauce, tossing over low heat. Finish with the reserved 3 tablespoons of extra virgin olive oil.

SERVES 2

Baked Salmon with King Crab
and Black Truffle Mashed Potatoes

2 tablespoons kosher salt

1 tablespoon sugar

1 bunch fresh dill

1 pound salmon fillets

½ pound Idaho potatoes

4 tablespoons butter

¼ cup milk

¼ cup freshly grated Parmesan cheese

2 ounces black truffle

½ cup fresh crab meat, picked
    through, excess water squeezed out

Salt and freshly ground pepper
    to taste

Mix the kosher salt and sugar together. Reserve 4 sprigs of dill to use as garnish. Pick the remaining dill off the stems and chop it. Spread the dill over the flesh side of the salmon fillets. Sprinkle the salt and sugar mixture evenly on top. Cover the top side only of the seasoned salmon with plastic wrap. Place the salmon on a slotted or perforated sheet with another sheet (like the broiler pan) underneath to catch draining water, and refrigerate it for 6 to 8 hours (no more, or it will get too salty). When you're ready to make dinner, brush the seasoning off the salmon, then rinse the fillets quickly and pat them dry. Slice the fillets diagonally into 4 pieces. In a hot non-stick skillet on medium heat, sear them for about 4 minutes per side, making sure to do the skin side first.

Just before searing the salmon, boil the potatoes in a pot of lightly salted water until they're fork tender, about 10 to 12 minutes. Drain them, peel them, and pass them through a food mill or ricer. Return the mashed potatoes to the pot over very low heat. Add the butter, milk, and Parmesan cheese, beating vigorously with a wooden spoon. Shave the truffle. Reserve a few shavings to use as garnish, and chop the remainder. Stir the chopped truffle and the crab meat into the potatoes, beating until smooth. Adjust the seasoning with salt and pepper.

Mound the mashed potatoes in the middle of each of 2 plates. Lay the salmon pieces on top. Garnish with the reserved dill sprigs and truffle shavings.

SERVES 2

Simply Tuscan

282

Vin Santo Gelatin with Grapes

1 cup seedless green grapes
¼ cup walnut halves, each cut in
    half again
1 tablespoon golden raisins, soaked in
    ¼ cup Vin Santo for 1 hour to
    plump, then drained

Soak the gelatin in cold water until
it is soft. While the gelatin is soft-
ening, warm the 1¼ cups of Vin Santo
until it is around body temperature
(55° to 60°F.). When the gelatin is
soft, squeeze the water out of it and
add it to the warm Vin Santo. Add the
sugar and mix until the gelatin and
sugar are completely dissolved.

Pour one quarter of the Vin
Santo/gelatin mixture into a 1-quart
savarin mold, and place it in the
refrigerator to chill until firm,
about 30 minutes. When chilled, top
evenly with the grapes and raisins,
then pour the rest of the Vin
Santo/gelatin mixture on top. Return
to the refrigerator to chill until
firm, 2 to 3 hours. To unmold, dip the
mold briefly in hot water, then turn
it out onto a platter.

3 sheets gelatin
1¼ cups Vin Santo wine
¼ cup sugar

SERVES 2 TO 4

Index